Made in Shef
The Story of
JAMES DIXON & SONS
Silversmiths

Pauline Cooper Bell

Alistair Lofthouse
DESIGN &
PRINT

OF JAMES DIXON & SONS
CORNISH PLACE, SHEFFIELD

SILVER AND ELECTRO-PLATE
MANUFACTURERS

TRADE MARK

© Pauline Cooper Bell 2004

Designed by Alistair Lofthouse
Printed and published by:
ALD Design & Print
279 Sharrow Vale Road
Sheffield S11 8ZF

Telephone 0114 267 9402
E:mail a.lofthouse@btinternet.com

ISBN 1-901587-52-5

First published September 2004

TRADE MARK

Contents

TRADE MARK

Dedication

To my mother Mary Bell (nee Cooper) whose stories about her father and grandfather, Dixon employees, triggered my interest in Dixon's the Silversmiths. Sadly she died in 2003 just as I was beginning seriously to research the book.

To Barrie Cooper, my second cousin who together with his father, grandfather, and at least 3 previous generations spent virtually all of their working lives as employees of James Dixon's and Sons. Many of the stories and accounts of how things were done from the 1950's onwards came to me from Barrie.

Acknowledgements

With very special thanks to:

John Bradshaw, a local historian who gave all kinds of practical help and encouragement and who will one day write the definitive work on James Dixon's and Sons.

Peter, Sylvia and Christopher Perry of the silversmith's Perry and Glossop who helped me together with their staff to understand a lot more about the processes and tools used in producing EPNS and silver products. Peter was also at one time a Dixon's man and shared with me many artefacts, pictures and photographs some of which are reproduced in this book.

I would also like to thank the following people for their advice, cooperation, and permission to use photographs and in some cases for loans of material and or technical help:

Andrew Renwick, great nephew of Alfred Fawcett
Judith Farrar niece of Alfred Fawcett
Jackie Richardson, librarian Sheffield Assay Office
Staff in Sheffield archives
Bunty Hunt, daughter of Milo Dixon
Karen Lightowler, researcher Sheffield Flood
Pauline Jordan
George Foster-Jones, Site Manager, Cornish Place
Residents of Cornish Place in June 2004,
Phillips auctioneers (now a part of Bonhams)
Deborah Wheeldon
Roger Tetley
Graham Axley
Trevor Collins
Roger & Valerie Atkin
Gay Penfold
Smithsonian, Cooper-Hewitt, National Design Museum (Christopher Dresser photos)

TRADE MARK

Foreword

When James Dixon first started up in business almost 200 years ago, he could never have imagined how successful his firm would become, nor that its products would be known throughout the world.

Large family firms like Dixon's flourished in nineteenth century Sheffield, providing employment for thousands of workers. In the twentieth century they gradually disappeared. Much of their history has been lost, although many buildings like Cornish Place remain, now adapted to provide housing for a new breed of city-dwellers.

Many of the items made by Dixon's still survive in homes and collections throughout the world, a living testament to their Sheffield makers. The silver trade itself has not vanished from Sheffield. Craftsmen still cherish and use the skills passed on from one generation to the next to create beautiful silverware.

Interest in local history has grown over the years, as more and more people trace their family trees and want to find out more about their ancestors. However, not much has been published about the firms which employed large numbers of workpeople. This history of James Dixon's provides a fascinating glimpse into their lives.

Jackie Richardson

Sheffield Assay Office

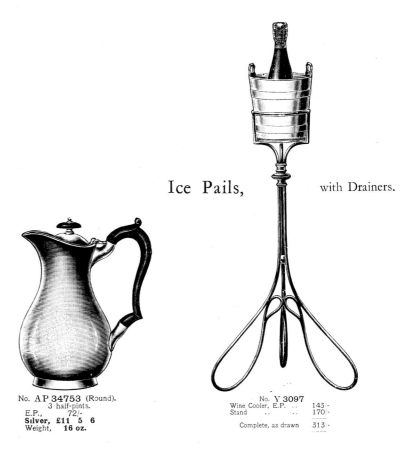

Ice Pails, with Drainers.

No. Y 3097
Wine Cooler, E.P. .. 143 -
Stand 170/-

Complete, as drawn 313 -

No. AP 34753 (Round).
3 half-pints.
E.P., 72/-
Silver, £11 5 6
Weight, 16 oz.

No. D 278
Sandwich Stand, 8 in., with loose pierced four-Division.
E.P. .. 40/-

TRADE MARK

v

Introduction

I was aware from being very young of the family link to Dixon's the silversmith's. We frequently walked along Dixon Rd and I knew our road, Dorothy Road, was linked in some way to the Dixon Family. I took on board that my grandfather was a silversmith and that he had, until he died in 1942, worked for Dixon's and lots of the relatives around where my grandmother lived in Hawthorn Rd worked for this same firm. There were objects around her house that had been made at Dixon's and these would lead to stories about my grandfather or his father. There were also old photographs.

The discovery after my grandmother's death of a marriage licence for a wedding in 1847 for a relative called Francis Cooper who according to the certificate was also a silversmith as was according to the same certificate, his father-in-law, got me into the family history.

When I finally had the time to seriously invest in research I decided that I wanted to look at Dixon's the firm as much as my own family. The stories seemed so interwoven. By that time the firm had closed but I was in contact with my Uncle Harry and his son Barrie both Coopers and both of whom had worked at Dixon's for most of their lives...more stories!

What I particularly wanted to do was to write a kind of history of Dixon's that included historical fact and even more that told the stories of the people, their experiences and the traditions that made this relatively small firm a world famous producer of silver and EPNS products. I wanted also to try to record something of the family stories, legends and myths relating to Dixon's. I think that these memories tell us much about the ethos and spirit of the communities that bred them. Most of the British population know little about King Alfred other than that he burnt the bread cakes. I think this is because this is something 'human', and it tells us about him as a person; this is the dreamer, the visionary lost in his own thoughts, frustrating for the cook but inspiring for the rest of us.

Much of what I have put on record was contained in the memories both of my own family, those related to the Dixon's, people who worked there, and also what I found in papers, letters and reflections in the Dixon's archived documents. I see the facts about dates and buildings as being the foundation or the skeleton but what I especially wanted, was to capture incidents that would show something of the 'the heart' of the firm.

I have chosen as the vehicle for this record the idea of working my way through the alphabet so that A is for Apprenticeship, B is for Burnishers, C is for Cooper's, a dynasty etc. This model has provided me with the needed hooks on which to build the story and has avoided any necessity to try to fit the stories into a perfect chronological order. I have kept it as a tool rather than allowing it to become a straight jacket so X for Xyonlyte, a material used for making knife handles was my way in to exploring something of the variety of materials used for handles and the skills of the hafter.

Quite late on in my research Graham Axelby lent to me a tape recording. This was his father's copy of a recording made by Sheffield Libraries around 1980. It is after Milo's death in 1976 though there was still some work going on at Cornish Place. One of the library staff interviewed Dick about his working life. In the tape he shares stories and experiences. Where in the text I quote Dick, the source would be this tape

I hope that the final version of the book is a contribution to the record of a firm and all those who ever belonged there who together provided the world with some remarkable works of art and craft as well as everyday utensils and tools for use in the home and on the sports field. Above all I hope that it is a reflection of 'the feel' and spirit of a firm that was at the centre of an important industrial period in the history of Sheffield's development as a world famous producer of cutlery and other metal products made of silver, steel and other alloys.

Apprenticeship

Barrie Cooper (right) and Walt Haynes, 1956-57, aged 17-18

The tradition of apprenticeship

Like all the trades that had established guilds during the middle ages, the metal trades which increasingly dominated Sheffield's employment scene trained boys and in later years girls through some kind of apprenticeship scheme. In many instances this was a parent to child relationship though there were instances when established craftsmen would take on boys from other families with whom they had connections or contacts.

By the second half of the 1800's Dixon's had become an established firm. The very first apprentice was reputed to be a John Butcher 'a native of Derbyshire' though how he came to Dixon's is not recorded (1). The usual route of parent to child training can be clearly seen in my own family. According to the 1851 census my great-great-great-grandmother Martha Barber was a burnisher as were her two daughters, Ann and Mary. I assume that their mother or a colleague of hers had taught Mary and Ann my great-great-grandmother, the 'trade'. Martha's grandson, my great grandfather Henry also worked for Dixon's and presumably got his apprenticeship as a silver stamper through the influence of his mother. After his father's death or desertion when Henry was a child, she had remarried a John Buxton who was also a silver stamper. By 1881 they were living next door to one another in houses Henry had had built. It seems very likely that his stepfather taught Henry the trade. Henry's eldest son William or Billy was also a stamper and both his older sons went on to become skilled craftsman who worked for Dixon's.

Apprenticeship Controversy

Apprenticeships in the silver industry were very controversial around 1899-1902 when there was a widely publicised conflict between the unions and the owners of big concerns like Dixon's. In January 1900 an article appeared in the Sheffield Independent under the heading 'Silver trades difficulties in Sheffield'. (2)

As I understand it, there was at the time a shortage of labour and some firms started to recruit larger numbers of boys and place them in 'teams' under one skilled workman. An example was given of 12 boys in one team. The unions objected on the grounds that it was contrary to union rules and was not in the interests of the boys. In addition these employers were paying 25% less than respectable firms. There were fears in the union that such large numbers of recruits would ultimately flood the labour market and that in a time of recession there would be substantial unemployment.

At the first conference of Masters (Owners) and workman November 7th 1898 the masters asked for three things:

1. Branches that only admitted journeyman's sons or relatives to come into the trade should abrogate the rule
2. Masters should have apprentices under them as in past years and to this end all resolutions should be rescinded which provided that apprentices should be under one workman only
3. Masters to have a free hand in matter of number of boys.

The unions, who first proposed a scheme of 1 boy to 8 men and then 1 boy to 6 men, resisted the latter stoutly. At the second conference the master's suggested 1 boy to 2 men and that the boys should be apprenticed to the masters. It was argued by the unions that this scheme meant the masters got rich and that it was 'ruinous to the workmen'. The master would get £100 profit by direct payment out of every boy working for the firm and on going indirect profit. The men who got no financial profit from the scheme did the training of boys voluntarily.

TRADE MARK

The employers issued a circular in December 1899 claiming agreement with the unions that 'Apprentices would not be placed under men of less than 25 years and that not more than one apprentice would be placed under one workman unless other workman in the same employ did not wish to take apprentices and a committee of three men to be appointed by the employees in each factory was suggested to watch over the workman's interests and to report to the employer where necessary.'

The whole dispute rumbled on and the masters withdrew their offer when the union would not agree to the masters having a freehand in the introduction of the conditions sited in the circular. They demanded:

1. Every apprentice to be bound under indenture to one man
2. Each man to have only one apprentice
3. A workman must be 25 before he could take on an apprentice and the percentage of men to boys to be agreed in order to meet the demands of normal trade
4. A joint committee of equal numbers of employers to workman to be set up to deal with points of difference arising
5. A small committee to be set up in each works who would watch the progress of the boys during apprenticeship and report to the masters and/or the committee any irregularities or injustice.

The Independent on November 21st 1901 commented that:' the team system in both stamping, buffing and finishing is a great evil and ought to be abolished. Every man should receive whatsoever his abilities will enable him to earn and no workman should sweat his brother...it is wrong for one man to take out work by piece and get it done at a less price'

It is recorded in a Dixon's minutes book (4) that on March 14th 1902, 54 people handed in their notice. I think this was notice of strike action rather than resignation. Each is listed. No comment is made and in that book no explanation of what subsequently happened. According to Pollard (5) there was a 5 month strike of silversmiths in 1900 and a 3 month strike of Britannia metal smiths in 1902 which led to wage increases and the establishment of an arbitration board in return for the abolition

Barrie Cooper and Tony Ashton, 1956-57, aged 17-18

of the ban on masters' apprenticeships. It seems like the length of the dispute led to issues becoming somewhat confused! Whether the strike continued for that length of time at Dixon's I am unable to tell from the archive material but it would surprise me if the firm could have survived such a lengthy strike and continued to maintain it's reputation. By 1904 it must have been preparing for its' centenary celebrations and such a long dispute would surely have undermined its success and employer employee relationships. I have not found any evidence of this.

Moving on to February 1st 1919 an arrangement was made by Mr. Fawcett, (the firm was jointly owned by the Dixon and Fawcett families), for each women burnisher to take an apprentice and for the firm to be responsible for apprentice wages for a period of 18 months. Then the women who had a girl were to pay part of the wages, 'the amount to be decided nearer the time of expiration of 18 months'(6). The mothers of girls were promised a 1/- a year advance and the wage to be 7/- a week plus 30%, this being wartime scale only. On February 20th 3 more women are recorded as agreeing to take girls on these terms. After the war the wage became 5/- a week plus 75% bonus. This gave them a wage of 8/9d a week.

In the same source it is recorded that all girls 'employed at Mr. Harvey's sink or the boiling out sink are paid for holidays but when they are placed as an apprentice with a 'piecework' polisher or burnisher they cease to be paid for holidays. Girls remaining with Mr Harvey are paid until they are out of their time'.

Rates of pay 1945 onwards
In the mid 1950's (1952-58) one of my relatives started work at Dixon's. The conditions under

which he was taken on were very similar to those proposed during the dispute. In theory at least Barrie was bound for 6 years from leaving school at 15 to his 21st birthday. Some people did break this particularly if the period in question was interrupted by 'National Service' call up. His wages were 2 guineas a week and were increased every 6 months so that by the time he was 21 he was earning 6 guineas a week. In fact the apprenticeship pay scales agreed in 1945 (7) stated that the apprentices were to receive a percentage of the minimum rates of adult workers, according to their age and not their stage in the apprenticeship. The scale was at

Age 15	27.5%
Age 15/6	30%
Age 16	32.5%
Age 16/6	35%
Age 17	40%
Age 17/6	45%
Age 18	50%
Age 18/6	55%
Age 19	60%
Age 19/6	67.5%
Age 20	77%
Age 20/6	87.25%
Age 21	Full min. wage

All were to be employed by the firm. An adult worker could have up to 5 apprentices but in the same department there could be only one per every other remaining adult.

Barrie's experience
When Barrie left school his father Harry Cooper took him, already the 5th generation of the family to work for Dixon's, to see Mr. Constantine, the works manager. Mr Constantine or Connie (as he was usually known to the workers) had a formidable reputation. I imagine that today his manner of relating might from Barrie's feeling about him be classed as bullying at work. He was certainly intimidating.

Mr. Constantine explained that there were 4 vacancies for apprentices. It seems from this that the 'Masters', who in this sense are the employers, had control over the numbers. Barrie was to go and have a look round with his father and see which one of the apprenticeships he would like to take up. Harry had already had a word with a man called Wilf Gorman who like Harry was a finisher though Harry specialised in hollow-ware and Wilf in 'spoon and fork'. Barrie says he had a free choice and chose to work with Wilf, which meant that he would become a finisher like his father.

Towards the end of the apprenticeship when a fairly high level of skill had been achieved it was common practice if things were a bit slack for the skilled workman to go home and leave the apprentice to finish a job. In Barrie's experience Wilf would indicate how much work he expected Barrie to get through in the rest of the working day. Barrie (and presumably others) accepted this as a way of paying the workman back for teaching you the skills of the trade. It was however contrary to the earlier union proposal though it did mean that the skilled workman profited certainly as much as the master or owner of the firm. My great-grandfather by the time he died aged 80 in 1928 had built 5 houses. I often wondered how as a silver stamper he had managed to achieve this and Barrie's father Harry suggested that he had profited through the extra work done by his apprentices over the years as a part of the piecework agreements. If this were the case it was happening for at least twenty years before the dispute because he built his first house in 1878.

During Barrie's apprenticeship the firm was hit by import bans to Australia and New Zealand. Markets were lost particularly for flatware. When things got slack Barrie went for a while to work with Harry who had an elderly very unwell colleague. Harry was a specialist hollow-ware finisher (hollow-ware being almost everything else except cutlery) so Barrie was then able to finish both types of products.

One of Barrie's early memories of learning the trade is the severe ache that he got in the shoulders from holding the product on the 'wheel'. With just a short break Barrie was to continue this trade until Dixon's closed down in the late 1980's and even after that he did part-time work for a younger ex colleague who had set up a small firm in the same area of Sheffield as Dixon's factory was in.

Harry did the job for over 50 years, retiring when he was 67 when he was working only part time. The firm was beginning to shed workers in 1971 as demand for products lessened. Nevertheless apprentices were still being recruited in this year and subsequent years and Sheffield Archives holds a box of actual signed agreements for the 1970's, which is subject to the data protection act. (8) However I do have a copy of what was signed up to which seems to have changed very little during the twentieth century.

Disillusionment with the apprenticeship scheme?

Although boys were still going into these traditional type schemes as late as the 1970's, I believe that for many young men they seemed a tedious option. Another of my second cousins, Terrance Cooper was an apprenticed silversmith at Dixon's just after World War 2. According to company records (9) he was a seriously promising apprentice, winning in 1950 some kind of scholarship to Sheffield College of Art. He followed this up by winning first prize for a silver fruit bowl which he made by hand. However he went during his apprenticeship to do National Service and I guess this opened up his horizons. He became interested in outdoor pursuits and pursued as far as I know a career working with young offenders and then in the security branch of the civil service working in various British embassies. It was unrealistic to expect such young men to return to an apprenticeship with no expectation of a full status until they were aged 23. In any case the world had changed and other career possibilities than following family tradition were available to the many.

Sources

1   Sheffield Archives, Dixon's A73 Minutes Book 1844 (contains records up to 1902 and several other documents)
2   Sheffield Independent January 5th 1900 'Silver Trades Difficulties in Sheffield', The Apprenticeship Question.
3   Sheffield Archives, Dixon's A73 Minutes Book 1844 (contains records up to 1902 and several other documents)
4   Ibid
5   Pollard Sidney A History of Labour in Sheffield, Liverpool University Press 1959 p.221
6   Sheffield archives, Dixon's A134, Apprenticeship Registration Forms 1970-74)
7   Sheffield Archives Dixon's A195 Volume marked 'Cash Book', but containing memoranda and notes 1952-62'
8   Sheffield Archives, Dixon's A192, Notebook containing extracts from documents, notes or memoranda, abstracts from agreements etc 1896-1923
9   Sheffield Archives Dixon's A199 Volume of Notes and memoranda marked matters of interest 1945-52

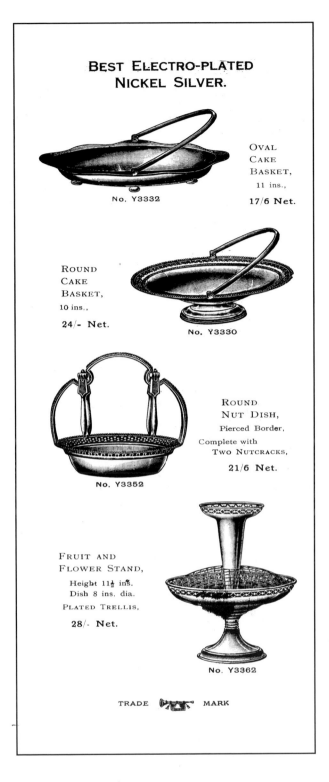

BEST ELECTRO-PLATED NICKEL SILVER.

No. Y3332

OVAL CAKE BASKET, 11 ins., 17/6 Net.

ROUND CAKE BASKET, 10 ins., 24/- Net.

No. Y3330

No. Y3352

ROUND NUT DISH, Pierced Border, Complete with TWO NUTCRACKS, 21/6 Net.

FRUIT AND FLOWER STAND, Height 11½ ins. Dish 8 ins. dia. PLATED TRELLIS, 28/- Net.

No. Y3362

TRADE MARK

TRADE MARK

Burnishers and Finishers

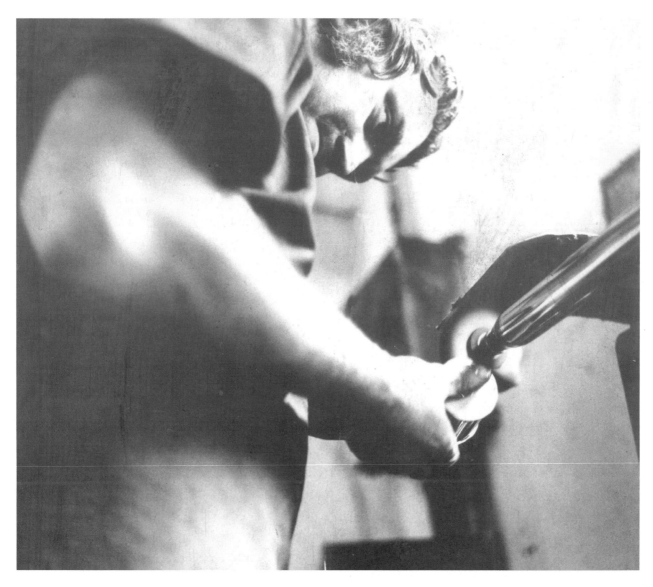

Barrie Cooper in 1974. The spindle can be clearly seen.

Burnishers in the family

I have long suspected that my great great grandmother Ann worked for Dixon's. I discovered early on in my research when looking at the 1851 census that she, her mother Martha Barber and her sister Mary Barber were employed as burnishers. Although Ann had married in 1847 and had a son Henry, she was according to the census widowed by 1851. Assuming she gave up work when she married and also because of the pregnancy she obviously returned to work at some point presumably to earn enough to keep herself and her child. She also returned to live with her mother and sister.

The direct link to Dixon's is evidenced by the fact that Martha and Mary Barber were in 1865 paid 5/- compensation each for loss of time resulting from damage caused by the Sheffield Flood of 1864 when the Dales Dyke reservoir broke its banks. They are listed amongst other workers in a Schedule of compensation. (1) Ann was by this time remarried and back working at Dixon's as a burnisher. Her new husband also worked for the firm.

Burnishing seems to have been mostly done by women and was the final process in the production of silverware.

Barrie Cooper with a finished fish platter which was a special order for an Arab Sheik's yacht.

How is it done?

In the Dixon's Centenary Souvenir booklet, there is a photograph of the burnishing room showing a room full of women sitting at long workbenches. (2). As far as I understand the process it was intended to give the product its' highly polished finish and also conceal any of the inevitable impurities. The piece was cleaned and then coated with soft soap. A mixture of sand and water were rubbed in to remove any grease and dirt. To remove scratches an agate

Burnishing Room 1905 - Note the women on the front, girls on the back.

burnisher was moved back and forth over the metal by hand. A steel burnisher closed the pores of silver and the gleaming finish was achieved by the use of bloodstone and finally wet rouge polished with a soft old linen cloth. According to the Centenary booklet (1905) it took a whole day to burnish an ordinary teapot. In the process of making a silver plated article today, a burnisher would not really have a place. The finisher might use a burnishing tool which looks a bit like a cross between a screwdriver and a chisel to cover a defect in the electroplating or the silversmith might likewise seal a blemish where two parts of say a teapot had been joined.

What was burnished?

In Sheffield Archives there is a 'Burnishers' Price Book 1868' (3). At the beginning of the book is a list of products that went through the hands of the burnishers. These are listed alphabetically and begin with:

Baskets Cake
Baskets Sugar
Beakers

Bottle stands through a huge variety of products to tea and coffee sets to wine strainers. All had their price. (see section on 'Pay'). At this stage all would have been done by hand.

In Mr Constantine's notes (4) for 1937 is a list of employees who had served more than 50 years there were 26 in all, 4 of them women, a total of 1,258 years. The purpose of gleaning this information was a challenge issued by the Sheffield Independent to find firms with long serving employees. They featured from Dixon's Mrs Guy (Dec 8th 1937) then aged 73, a burnisher who had no time off for illness in her 59 years with the firm. She is quoted as saying 'When I came to the firm there were about 60 burnishers in the department (EPNS). But now we only have 13 or 14...I came as an apprentice for 3 years but nowadays the girls will not come like I did' The paper went on to say:

Mrs Guy irons, polishes and brings up the surfaces of the goods after they have been plated. Apparently the only change since she had entered the trade was the introduction of mechanical mops. She worked an 11hour day. Her picture can be seen in the section on Relationships where she is presenting a tankard to Mr Lennox.

TRADE MARK

Finishers

As the twentieth century progressed, the process became more mechanised. It is my guess that with the advent of machines the job began to be done by men and that by the middle of the century what had been done by women burnishers was later mostly done by finishers. I suspect there is a bit of social history here in that polishing was women's work and machinery made it into men's work! My Uncle Harry who worked for Dixon's for 50 years (1927-1971) was a hollow-ware finisher and his son Barrie began as an apprentice flatware finisher but also trained to finish hollow-ware. Incidentally, Harry in order to pay off his mortgage when he first got married did a day's work at Dixon's and followed it by doing the evening shift at Batchelor's canning factory! He was 67 when he retired.

The finishers operated a machine that had spindles that rotated and to which the finisher attached different fittings according to the size of the product being worked on and the stage in the process. The attachments, known as dollies or buffs were made of different materials, some very hard that were known as scratch brushes and some that were softer made of a textile such as calico or swan's down which would give the product its' mirror like gleam after the plating process.

Harder dollies were usually used before the product was plated and at this stage the process was originally called liming after the 'lime' that was used as a cleaning agent. A substance called 'compo' and black rouge that must have been slightly more 'healthy' for the finisher's lungs replaced this product in later years. Finishing required enormous skill. Too much rubbing with a hard dolly could scar and since it was after the plating stage the silver might disappear so very soft dollies were then used! Smaller dollies were needed to get under handles on products like jugs where as waiters could be worked on with dollies or buffs that had a large circumference. The whole process required fine judgement and lightness of touch. Very small marks or 'pits' would be 'doctored' or 'ragged'. The tool like a very small chisel (a buffer?!)

would be cleaned by holding it on the turning spindle for a few seconds as would the area to be worked on and the 'pit' would then be gently rubbed with the buffer tool to work just enough surrounding silver into it to fill it up. Occasionally a product was finished off by hand burnishing. Any product, which was wirework like a cruet, would never be finished but would be burnished.

Buffing

Buffing came at an earlier stage before the silver plate was applied and traditionally, women buffed flatware and men hollow-ware. Buffing was a really dirty process as the products used were a mixture of pumice and oil. Hence the traditional pictures of buffers covered by brown paper as well as aprons and smocks. My Uncle Edwin Cooper was a hollow-ware buffer.

The machinery for both buffing and finishing could be dangerous. Harold Cooper was the youngest son of old Henry Cooper and was a hollow-ware buffer. Harold once had an accident. He was removing the buff from the spindle and the spindle went right through the centre of his hand. However he survived long enough to become a member of the 'teapot club'. After 50 years of service employees were presented with a teapot and Harold was given his, suitably inscribed, on August 2nd 1946.

Shortages of Buffers

After World War 2 it became increasingly difficult to recruit buffers and men began to do the job. In October 1945 the management tried to discuss with the existing women buffers why they did not want to work full time. Some of the married ones said they wanted time to do the shopping. And others did not want to earn more than £2/14/- a week or they then had to pay income tax. The firm offered a 10% bonus on a weekly wage of more than £3. However the writer (5) noted that this had become an expensive method of production 'seeing that 5 men were required to control 29 women'! Women buffers were a formidable crowd and seriously intimidated many of the men. A lot of men would not go into a workshop unless another man was with them. By 1961 there was still a shortage of buffers.

Lily White in the 1930's buffing spoons, note that she is working on 4 or so spoons at the same time.

Rates of pay for the finishers and buffers were by the twentieth century negotiated by the unions though the basic pricing system was as for the burnishers with the added sophistication of bonuses that were a percentage of piecework money earned. In practice the workers would ask for a bit more if the job was for some reason a little more difficult than the norm. In essence they were on piecework and Barrie preferred that to being 'datal' i.e. being paid a daily rate though there was a basic rate 'on clock' as a Dixon's employee to which was added the piecework incentive. On piecework Barrie felt he was his own boss. It gave him and others the freedom to decide that if they had earned enough wages for that week they might negotiate an afternoon off. Barrie can remember when the film 'Star Wars' first came out going with a workmate to see it in the afternoon rather than queue in the evening. He had earned what he needed to for the week. However it seems they would not have done this if there had been pressure on Dixon's to complete an order by a particular date. Workers felt loyalty and had a commitment to the firm.

Scratch Brushers

Scratch brushers were usually women whose job was to deal with the insides of products like teapots or coffeepots. The firm's handyman would go with a flat barrow to the local brewery that was just round the corner from Cornish Place. He would bring back a couple of barrels of stale beer, which were then poured, into a vat. The 'brush' was dipped into this and then fixed to a spindle rather like the finisher fitted on his buffs. It was then used to scour the inside of the pot leaving a clean relatively smooth surface but without the shine. Mr Constantine commented in the 1940's that a shortage of scratch brushers was holding up the production of goods that the firm were trying to make to beat threatened overseas import bans

When the work was finished.

Once workers had finished a job they took it to the warehouse where the job was booked and dated. This procedure proved you had done the work. The work was booked in each Wednesday and the workers were paid on the Friday. A book with carbon copies was used. The work done was recorded in the book and the worker was given the top copy.

Presumably this is how Barrie's parents met as his mother before she married Harry worked in

Dixon's EPNS warehouse from the age of 14. Her name was Lottie May Taylor and they had 'an understanding' for several years before they got married.

Sources

1   Sheffield archives, Dixon's A254 Inundation Compensation to workman for loss of time. September 28[th]1865
2   Centenary souvenir James Dixon & Sons, Sheffield 1906 p.29
3   Sheffield Archives, Dixon's B535 Burnishers' Price Book 1868
4   Sheffield Archives, Dixon's A188 Volume marked S Constantine random notes of some interest 1936-39
5   Sheffield Archives Dixon's A195 Volume marked 'Cash Book', but containing memoranda and notes 1952-62'

Ada Jennings, Scratch Brusher

Knife Rests. Priced per pair,

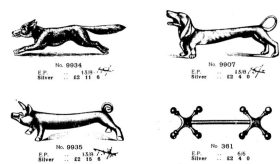

No. 9934
E.P. Silver .: 13/8 .: £2 11 6

No. 9907
E.P. Silver .: 13/8 .: £2 4 0

No. 9935
E.P. Silver .: 13/8 .: £2 15 6

No. 361
E.P. Silver .: 6/6 .: £2 4 0

TRADE MARK

Coopers - A Dynasty

Old Henry Cooper, Silver Stamper with wife Emma

Henry Cooper (1847-1928) worked at Dixon's, silversmiths in Cornish Place all of his life. I believe that both his parents also worked there and his grandparents. His father Francis or Frank was, according to his marriage certificate, a silversmith and his mother Ann (nee Barber) is recorded in the 1851 census as a burnisher. I believe Francis was the first of the Coopers to go into a metalwork trade as his father who died when Francis was about 14 was in fact a miller and merchant with a substantial business dealing in corn, ale and tea.

Henry's parents were, I imagine married in somewhat of a hurry in August 1847, out of parish (Dronfield). Henry was born in November. The family lived in Chester Street at the time of his birth but by 1851 only Henry and his mother appear on the census returns and they are living with Martha Barber, Ann's mother and Mary, Ann's younger sister in Robert St. Charles Barber, Martha's husband was a silversmith according to his daughter's marriage certificate so it seems a reasonable assumption that he also worked at Dixon's. I believe that Francis and Ann met through their work at Dixon's.

Ann remarried and John Buxton was a silver stamper. Henry married in May 1869. His new wife was Emma Firth whose father William is described as a steel connector or convertor. Family tradition believes there is a link to the famous Firth steel-making firm for which my own father worked in the 1940's Firth Brown's. At the time of the marriage Henry was 21 and Emma 19. Their marriage was to last 59 years and he died just 8 months before Emma in 1928. Together they had 6 children: Frances (girl) (and again is this a link to Henry's father Francis?), Annie, Billy, Minnie, Henry (my grandfather) and Harold. I think that they also lost a son as a child, Charles. All the boys eventually worked at Dixon's

Property Developer?
Henry and Emma seemed to have had a financially very successful marriage in the context of the late 19th early 20th century particularly given the number of children.

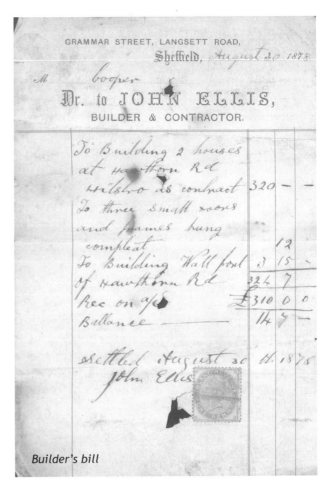

Builder's bill

Dixon's was in Sheffield 6 and at first Henry and Emma lived in Woodland Street and then in 1878 he had two houses built in Hawthorn Rd. These were paid for in instalments to the builder John Ellis. On June 20th Henry paid £80, followed within the next two months by instalments of a further £60, £80 and £60. The account was settled on August 30th when he paid the balance of £14.7s to make a grand total for two houses of £310. In 1883 he had a kitchen added at the back at right angles to the living room and a greenhouse was attached to the end of the kitchen. I still have the architect's plans for this work. At a much later date probably in the time of his son's ownership a bathroom was added over the top of the kitchen that was accessed through a bedroom. I seem to remember when I was a child, (1950ish) the installation of an inside toilet into this bathroom which meant there was no longer a need to use the outside toilet at the bottom of the garden.

On June 20th 1882 Henry signed an agreement to buy a plot of land, (plot 90) from the Hillsborough Freehold Land Society. There is no record of what he paid but the conveyancing costs were £4.4s. I believe that these were a further 2 houses so that he owned four terraced houses all of which shared the same backyard. (Nos. 65-59) Hawthorn Rd. Until my grandmother and Aunt died in the 1960's when my mother inherited and sold No 65, three out of the four were still occupied by his descendants. To day **each** would be valued at more than £80,000

Later on he either had built or bought houses in Fielding Rd. At one time all the land these roads were built on was part of the Dixon Estate in Hillsborough, Sheffield.

I think that all these houses in modern terms were Henry's pension and that some at least were rented out to his children. When both he and Emma died Emma being the surviving partner, each of the children were left under the terms of the will, the house in which they lived and one other. Henry and Harold had the Hawthorn Rd properties and the daughters, properties in Fielding Rd where they lived. Billy was already dead so his widow Rosetta also got a Fielding Rd. property as long as she remained a widow and if she remarried it was to be sold and the proceeds given to her children. Some family arrangement must have been made as Rosetta continued to live in Hawthorn Rd in what had

Henry Cooper Junior, worked as silversmith at Dixons for nearly 50 years. Died in 1942, aged 62.

been her family home (No 59) but which under the terms of Emma's will now belonged to Harold. One of her son's Frank lived in this house when he got married and Rosetta moved next door to the smaller property where she lived with her eldest son Edwin.

Where did Henry and Emma get their money? I would have expected the acquisition of this number of properties to be beyond the means of a silver stamper employee at Dixon's in the late nineteenth century. It is possible Emma brought some money to the marriage. However Harry my uncle and son of Billy said that Henry always had apprentices and these apprentices would each reach a stage when they were doing high quality work for which Henry was getting paid. Assuming the system of remuneration was on piecework terms of employment, there must have been times when he was bringing in more than the average weekly wage.

TRADE MARK

*Edwin Cooper, Hollow-ware Buffer,
outside 63 Hawthorn Road, 1940s*

*Harold Cooper (left) worked for Dixon's as a
Hollow-ware Buffer for 54 years and Harry Cooper,
Hollow-ware finisher, started at Dixon's in the 1920s.*

His Descendants

All of Henry's sons worked for Dixon's including Henry my grandfather. He had only daughters and I imagine at that time that women in works like Dixon's did less skilled jobs so the tradition was not maintained and the daughters trained for more secretarial type roles. However two out of the three of Billy's sons went into the firm, Harry mentioned above and Edwin. Frank for some reason worked for Arnold Laver as a carpenter. Harry's son Barrie worked for Dixon's except for a brief interlude until he was made redundant when the firm closed. He did up to retirement age occasional bits of work for an ex-colleague who I believe would be described as a 'little mester'. Barrie lives in Hillsborough and has now reached retirement age. The tradition even had Dixon's still been in business would have died out as Barrie has no children.

Family Dynasties

It seems that the Coopers were typical of many families whose skills were passed down from father to son. Failing that it was possible for the family connection to be used to obtain employment within the firm and the young person would be apprenticed to an experienced workman willing to take him on. This must have been the experience of old Henry. His stepfather

was John Buxton who had married Ann and he was a silver stamper. He therefore must have been apprenticed to his stepfather. By the time Edwin and Harry his grandsons wanted apprenticeships their father was dead so again either old Henry or the boys' uncles (Henry, my grandfather or Harold) got them into the firm.

Whilst I believe that this kind of continuity of service and length of family involvement was unusual Barrie is aware of family's who were there when he started his working life at Dixon's who had 3 generations of experience at least. He recalls two families in particular the Lindley's and the Baxter's who were spoon and fork buffers. It was a Lindley who was reputed to be the first to use a lathe for buffing spoons. (2) Another dynasty was that of the Bingham's. In the 1906 centenary celebration programme is a list of all the current employees. In this list there are 7 Bingham's, 4 Coopers, 6 Baxter's and 11 Lindley's. The centenary brochure also refers to the Heeleys, 3 generations of whom served as the firm's representative in Scotland and the North East of England.

In Sheffield Archives amongst Milo Dixon's papers is a newspaper cutting about the retirement of Charlie Baxter on 13th Oct. 1972. He was a silversmith, lived in Providence Rd, Walkley and was 90 years of age having worked at Dixon's since 1895. When he started he said the hours were 6a.m. until 8p.m. He wanted it to be known that he was only retiring because of his wife's ill health.

Barrie remembers Charlie as a real character and said his longevity was certainly not due to healthy living! He liked a drink or two, took snuff and Barrie thinks he also smoked a pipe and had certainly fathered at least 7 children.

Sources

1 Sheffield Archives, Dixons B447 Papers of Milo Dixon 1962-75 incl. memoranda book 1962-75.

2 Sheffield archives, Dixon's A73 Minute Book 1844

3 Photocopy of the Programme of the Centenary Celebration Event 1906, (Bell family archives).

Cooper - Barber Family Associated with Dixon's

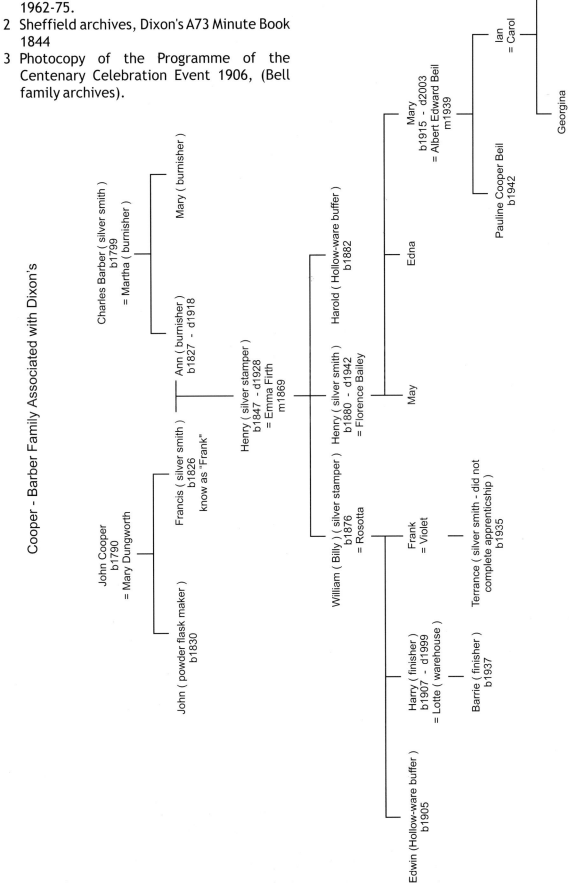

TRADE MARK

Dixon's the Firm

The beginnings

The Minute Book of 1844 (1) begins with a handwritten account by Thomas Wolstenholme which states that these statistics gathered in 1850 are obtained from manufacturers' books, trades union records and general information from the aged workman 'as nearly correct as could be got.'

	1805	1810	1820	1830	1840	1850
Manufactures	8	10	12	10	13	26
Workman	31	48	99	124	216	232
Boys	19	45	91	64	68	122

There is in the memoranda book of Milo Dixon (2) a photocopy of an 1828 trade directory, which cites the firm as ' Dixon and Son, manufacturers of Britannia Metal goods, spoons, patty tins, scallop shells etc, Cornish Place'. By 1873 the product range had increased to 32, the workmen to 335 and there were 112 boys. During this period Dixon's were the largest employers in the Britannia metal trade, having at least twice as many men as their nearest rivals. By 1893 the minute book records 670 employees. According to the centenary booklet of 1906(3) the employees numbered 900 persons and various catalogues would suggest that the product range was into the hundreds. There were showrooms not only at Cornish Place in Sheffield but also by the 1870's in Ludgate Hill in London.

By chance I recently came across an article about the formation of the Sheffield Gas Company in 1818(4) Listed amongst the shareholders some of whom are individuals and others firms, is Dixon & Smith. This would suggest they were very forward thinking.

Thomas Wolstenholme's account states that James Vickers in 1769 purchased for 5/- 'the receipt for making white metal'. Dixon's however is credited as beginning as a partnership in 1806 in Silver Street between James Dixon and Smith. 'The aged workman, according to Thomas, said that the first articles made were buckles for shoes and spoons cast in sand that for a time 'were got up without buffing' but were later buffed on lathes worked by foot. William Lindley employed as a handler of teapots was said to be the first to buff spoons on such a lathe.

Then followed beakers, tobacco and snuffboxes, coffee, sugar and cream receptacles. Silversmiths who had previously made light plated goods made these products and these men were known according to Thomas 'by the appellation of *shadow smilers*'.

The first trade directory that I have found in which Dixon's' has an entry is Banes (1822) which cites Dixon and Smith as manufacturers of Britannia metal goods and dealers in cutlery etc.

and gives their address as '16 Silver Street, proprietors of Rolling Mill, Green Lane'.

Cornish Place
In 1820 the firm moved about a mile to the buildings in Cornish Place and Ball Street. An article from a local paper around 1959-60 found in a works' journal suggested that the name Cornish was derived from the link to Britannia metal which was one of the first imitation alloys of silver and was made of 90% tin which came from Cornwall.

Dixon family members 1905

Milo also states that in 1931 the firm bought some second hand German machines that revolutionised the production of spoons and forks.

Milo writing in 1969 (6) also mentioned that many years ago they had taken over a firm called 'Muzzle' who made gun and cartridge loading implements. This was a key component of the business. In 1946 they took over G&JW Hawksley who made pocket flasks, ram rods and pull throughs and this business was merged with Dixon's flask department in 1956. (See chapter on Guns).

In 1821 the partnership with Smith came to an end and James' son William Fredrick joined the firm. The new partnership was formalised in 1825 with a seven-year deed of co-partnership to create James Dixon and Son (5). Other members of the family including in 1828 William Fawcett who had married James' daughter very soon became part of the business and so James Dixon and Sons was established into a formal partnership between these three and James Willis Dixon in 1836. In 1830 Dixon had acquired the firm of Nicholson, Ashforth and Cutts and began to produce silver and plated goods. William Fawcett managed this side of the business.

Spoons and forks and knives became the real bread and butter of the business and were definitely made very early on and certainly prior to 1861 which according to an account written by Milo Dixon in July 1969 were listed in their earliest surviving catalogue of 1861. Stainless steel was introduced into the trade in the 1920's and Dixon's were amongst the firms who switched to this metal for cutlery and some hollow-ware products. Stainless steel didn't tarnish like products made from other metal alloys.

Other catalogues illustrate a huge range of household and luxury goods that were developed during the latter part of the Victorian era

James Dixon and Sons Limited Company
The firm became a limited company on 16th July 1920 with a nominal capital of £200,000 in £1 shares. The holders were Ernest Dixon Fawcett and Lennox Burton Dixon (7). This reflected and continued the previous joint ownership of the firm between the Dixon and Fawcett families. The firm continued to trade as James Dixon and Sons and Lennox and Ernest were directors.

Lottie, Barrie's mother remembered Lennox Dixon from when she was a girl. He arrived at work each morning in a horse drawn hansom cab. The horse's hoofs used to clatter over the cobbles in the Dixon's yard so that every-one knew when he had arrived. Lennox managed the firm for 50 years or more and was presented with the silver teapot. In addition he received a wireless set and a tankard. All 700 employees attended the ceremony that was held in December 1936. A fourteen-year-old buffer girl Ivy Gregory presented a bouquet to Mrs. Dixon.

SPOONS & FORKS

The NEW NICKEL ALLOY
which combines all the essentials for
DURABILITY AND **HARD WEAR**,
and for all Domestic Purposes is
STAINLESS.

WEAR DOES NOT IMPAIR ITS **COLOUR**

AND IT DOES

NOT TARNISH,
SAVES TIME, TROUBLE,
COST OF CLEANING,
AND LASTS A LIFETIME.

PRICES:		
No. 1090 Tea Spoons ...	...	12/-
„ 1091 Dessert Spoons	...	24/-
„ 1092 Table Spoons	...	33/6
„ 1093 Dessert Forks	...	24/-
„ 1094 Table Forks ...	...	33/6

JAMES DIXON & SONS, L
CORNISH PLACE, SHEFFIELD.

TRADE  MARK

The firm seemed to carry on in profit until the 1930's. Milo recorded in 1969 that Dixon's had taken over the firm of Hutton's of West Street in 1930-31, giving them preference shares. At this time they were beginning to loose ground and it seems probable that the taking over Hutton's was an attempt to boost the business. Milo recorded that the takeover had resulted in the acquisition of old and valuable dies and tools and some good customers. However further investigation suggests, that this takeover gave rise as most such mergers do, to all kinds of tensions.

The man who had been Hutton's managing director, Sydney Gibbs joined the Board of Directors of James Dixon's and continued to carry some responsibility for sales and marketing. There is some correspondence available between him and Lennox Dixon (8) who was at the time a director. It is obvious from letters that Sydney struggled to accept the situation and seemed frequently to suggest in letters to Lennox that retailers such as Harrod's and Jay's of Oxford Street felt Hutton's goods had always been superior to Dixon's. He seemed to be the one to hear the damaging rumours one of which suggested that the whole firm was closing down. This led to the distribution of a letter that was sent to all customers saying,

We have pleasure in informing you that an agreement has been made between ourselves and Messrs James Dixon and Sons Ltd of Cornish Place. Our Birmingham works will be retained and will manufacture for both concerns. It is intended to keep the sales side of the two businesses separate. The London showrooms of both businesses will be carried on as before. Mr. S.C. Gibbs, Managing Director of Messrs William Hutton and Sons Ltd has joined the Board of Messrs James W Dixon and Sons Ltd and any correspondence addressed to us at 11 Warwick Court, High Holbourn or to Cornish Place, Sheffield in connection with Messrs Hutton and Sons will receive prompt attention.

He complains later that decisions about sales representatives and so on were made whilst he was away and that such decisions could surely have waited until his return. Such decisions seem to be around salesmen carrying goods that were originally Hutton's and Dixon's so my guess is that the Dixon's executives did not share Sydney's enthusiasm for maintaining the distinctions.

Lennox said that it was urgent that Smith one of the reps. In question 'was equipped with a range of goods of both firms' There is further complaint from Sydney that the West End is being neglected in favour of the suburbs and that Hutton's travellers are being got rid of. He sees the West End as a barometer of reputation. This merger does illustrate the challenge of 'managing change' in organisations about which so much has been written in the last half of the twentieth century. By August 16th 1932 goods transferred from Hutton's to Cornish Place amounted to a gross value of £30,050.

In Lennox's papers there is another letter from Sydney that I think is an interesting contemporary account of retailing history. In June 1931, Sydney attempted to obtain a contract with Marks and Spencer's. He writes, *I think I was exceedingly lucky to get an interview as I not only saw their Managing Director Mr. Sieff but actually the great Mr Marks himself. There must have been at least fifty representatives waiting their turn...they want all the things marked with probably a suitable fancy name and stainless nickel'*

Changes in terms of employment

In 1937 changes were proposed to the working week which seemed to be acceptable to most of the workforce though I believe that they were probably initiated as a means of cutting production costs. The proposal was to change the working week from 5½ days to 5 days. A handwritten paper exists in which the proposal is outlined. The writer, probably Sydney Constantine states:

The advantages both economic and otherwise would meet with the favour of all concerned. It will of course be necessary to lengthen the working 5 days so that lost hours of the Saturday morning can be maintained. It should be remembered that the plant heating and other amenities are available on Saturday mornings just as on other days and that many of the plant users are not here to use same. In brief it is very rare even on normal working days (other than Saturdays) to find all the plant working at the same time...

During the winter months much saving would be made by not having to heat the factory (coal & steam) and also on many occasions saving with regard to lighting. (Note a foggy day costs something like £4 for light). In re-arranging the

No. L1998
E.P.N.S. Engine Turned Shaker
and 6 Glasses in Leatherette
covered Case, Satin and
velvet Lined
116/-

No. L399.
"Jigger" Measure
E.P.N.S. E.B.M. B.M.
7/3   6/3   4/-

No. D1902
E.P.N.S. Spices Dish
32/-

No. D73/1.
Cocktail Service
E.P.N.S. and Glass Shaker and 4 Glasses 78/-
"   "   "   6   "   "   }91/-
No. D73
(Loose frame—Tray may be used separately.)

No. D1334
Cocktail Service,
E.P.N.S. Shaker and 6 Glasses 180/-
"   "   "   4   "   "   }138/-
No. D1334/2

No. L2002
Lemon Squeezer,
E.P.N.S., 6/- each

No. D1334,
Cocktail Service,
E.P.N.S. Shaker and 6 Glasses 180/-
"   "   "   4   "   "   }138/-
No. D1334/2

No. D1335
Cocktail Service
E.P.N.S. Shaker and 4 Glasses
88/-

No. L400
Cocktail Measure,
E.P.N.S., Gilt inside,
15/6 each

No. L1988
1   1½ pints
E.P.N.S
and Glass 46/- 53/-

No. L2976C
E.P.N.S. and Glass
Shaker in Case,
33/-

No. L1976C/1
1   1½ pints
E.P.N.S.
and Glass 21/- 25/-
(Coloured Cock)

No. L2003
1   1½ pints
E.P.N.S. 50/- 64/-

No. L1990
1   1½ pints
E.P.N.S.
and Glass 52/- 61/-

No. L1992
1½ pints
E.P.N.S.
and Glass   35/-

No. 4
Cherry Forks (Drawn full size) Silver,   26/- per doz.
"   "   Gilt, 38/- per doz.
Case for 6 Forks, 3/- each

No. L2007
79/-

E.P.N.S. and
Glass Shaker and
6 Glasses (Coloured
Cock and Gilt Line on
edge and foot) in velvet and
Satin Lined Case

No. D110
Cocktail Service
E.P.N.S. Shaker and 6 Glasses, 138/-
"   "   "   4   "   "   }104/-
No. D110/1

TRADE [trade mark] MARK

Cocktail Shakers & Services

hours consideration will have to be taken of the varying hours which already obtain...

This seemed to be resolved to everyone's satisfaction by juggling with lunch hours and length of week day hours. The factory inspector also agreed, the regulations stipulating only the maximum length of time people could work before a break was legally binding. The proposals met this stipulation.

Beginnings of financial problems

In June1936 there is a reference to Japanese competition in relation to spoons and forks. Apparently 288,617 dozen were imported valued at £9825. and the tariff board was asked to increase duties.(9) In the same source concern is expressed about Viner's selling a solid silver waiter costing 28/6d. I can remember my father who was a Firth Brown's man at one time expressing huge contempt for Viner's importing partially made products and finishing them in Sheffield and thus undercutting the local manufacturers. Further mention is made of flatware in September and again in October when 384,018 dozen pieces of chrome plated flatware to a value of £11,533 gives rise to a further demand for an increase in tariffs.

There is a quotation in the front of a couple of the work's 'diaries' which reads:

There is hardly anything in the world that some man cannot make a little cheaper and the people who consider price only are this man's lawful prey. (10)

Opening of the new Assay Office, 13th April 1959.
Left to right: J. Hugh Neill(Master Cutler)
R.M. Harland (Assay Master) Milo Dixon(Guardian)
Sir Douglas Branson (Law Clerk)
Alderman John W. Holland J.P. (Lord Mayor)

In December1937 a resolution was registered at companies house whereby ordinary shares were reduced from £1 to 5/-. The writing was definitely on the wall.

Annual losses amounted to between £6657 and £27,726 in the years 1930-36. This does need to be seen against the economic and social changes of the time. In 1921 there was a huge slump in trade throughout the country with 2 million people unemployed. The First World War had thrown international trade into total confusion. Britain as the trading centre of the world was falling behind through lack of investment in machinery. The great depression lasted from 1929-1932 when unemployment soared to levels hitherto unknown. The American economy shrank by 40% and the effect on Europe was devastating. Many factories closed and this was the era of the Jarrow March. In that town alone 75% were unemployed. Britain came off the gold standard, a move that stimulated trade as exports became cheaper. By 1937, the year Dixon's began to get back into profit things nationally began to improve. The firm returned to profit for a few years. The other social factor, which I believe must have greatly affected the firm, was the decline in domestic servants following the First World War. Many of the products which Dixon's sold required high levels of maintenance in 'spit and polish' and people no longer had the household servants to carry out these tasks. This was a low wage area and people wanted higher wages and the slump impacted on the middle classes cutting their financial capacity to pay for domestic help in home or garden.

TRADE MARK

Post World War 2

In 1947 it is recorded that very many of the countries to which Dixon's had in the pre war period exported goods were introducing bans on imports. These are listed as Chile, Argentina, the Scandanavian countries, Australia and Iceland. Some of these had future dates and frantic attempts were made to get orders out to beat the deadlines but the shortage of skilled workers was a handicap and women buffers in particular started to move from firm to firm to get the best wages. In 1952 Australia banned imports which was a serious blow as turnover in this market alone had been £60,000 a year.

There were huge changes for any firm to take on board in this period. The introduction of 'Pay as You Earn' taxation and National Insurance contributions must have required more clerical staff. Legislation promoting health and safety was probably very necessary but was at the same time a drain on financial resources when turnover was decreasing. There seemed to be a shortage of skilled workers and few wanting to come into the industry. This increased the power of the workforce so that there were ever increasing demands for higher wages. There is an interesting comment in 1950. I think the writer is Sydney Constantine. He says that the workpeople view 'P.A.Y.E' and N.I. contributions as the responsibility of the employer. He observes *"if we are to be given so called benefits by the state (people need to see) that the responsibility of the carrying out must be shared by those who are to benefit from them."* (11) The whole feeling of this particular 'works diary' is of a struggle.

The management of the firm stayed in the hands of the Dixon family until the 1970's with the death of Milo and the retirement of Mr Fawcett, though the latter had only worked part-time since 1966 when Charles William Samwell (usually known as Bill) had become a director. He took over some of the tasks that Alfred Fawcett had been responsible for.

Milo was the 5th generation to be in management and joined the firm in 1919. Milo was well liked by most of the workers. Peter Perry remembers working with Joe Hampton, the odd woker (made grape scissors and similar articles) one Saturday morning. Joe was not overfond of work and Peter was told to keep an eye open for Milo. He says that this was easy because Milo had a little dog whom went where ever Milo went and the dog always arrived first! He spent a year getting to know the processes and the workforce. However he was really interested in the selling of finished goods and the retirement of James Dixon, great grandson of the founder enabled him to take over his role of promoting the firm at home and also overseas. He travelled the whole of Ireland twice a year from 1924-1965 and frequently helped the firm's regular sales team in Manchester, Liverpool and Scotland. It is recorded, possibly by Milo in the works diary(12) for February 25th 1976, 'Receiver appointed by the bank National Westminster at our request'. In October of that year there was a mortgage of charge taken out on the buildings for £60,000 to the Bristol Evening Post. Milo died in office on December 31st 1976. Company records are difficult to follow but it seems to have gone into liquidation in 1978 and then again in 1982 when some assets were sold to Mappin and Webb for £76,185. As well as having been a director of Dixon's Milo Dixon was at one time chair of guardians of the Sheffield Assay Company. In 1976 there were 162 employees and the wage bill was £360,182. No dividend was paid and the loss for the year was £79,700.

The 1970's onwards

Serious problems continued during the mid 1970's. In April1975 VAT was increased to 25% that had a crippling effect on a lot of manufacturing industry though this was halved a year later. Bill Samwell resigned in August 1978. The firm had virtually collapsed by 1982 with debts of over one million pounds. Only 57 employees were retained and parts of the site were let out to other concerns. There was a re-launch with 30 employees in 1984 but the decline was irreversible. The firm was eventually absorbed into British Silverware. Production limped on at Cornish Place until the building closed in 1992 with a staff about the size that it had been in 1806.

In many ways Dixon's was a symbol of much of what was happening elsewhere in the British Isles. In all historic manufacturing centres of which Sheffield was just one, engineering, textiles, pottery production and printing had provided employment for hundreds of people for more than a hundred years. In the 1980's manufacturing slumped from 52% of the economy to 32%, the unprofitable went to the wall and unemployment rose by leaps and bounds until in 1882 there were 3 million unemployed which was a worse situation than in

TRADE MARK

20

the great depression. (13) During this period, James Dixon's was just one of very many family firms which more or less disappeared or were absorbed into other businesses which meant that the ethos and traditions of the original family firm were lost.

Sources

1 Sheffield archives, Dixon's A73 Minute Book 1844
2 Sheffield Archives, Dixon's B447 Papers of Milo Dixon 1962-75 incl. memoranda book 1962-75.
3 Centenary souvenir James Dixon & Sons, Sheffield 1906 p.33
4 Sheffield Ancestors Sheffield and Dist FHS 2002, article *Establishing a Gaslight Company* p.33
5 Milo Dixon op cit
6 Milo Dixon op cit
7 Companies House fiche No 00169123 James Dixon & Sons Limited
8 Sheffield archives, Dixon's A186 Correspondence of Lennox Dixon
9 Sheffield Archives, Dixon's A188 Volume marked S.Constantine, random notes of some interest 1936-39
10 Sheffield Archives Dixon's A195 Volume marked 'Cash Book', but containing memoranda and notes 1952-62'
11 Ibid
12 Milo Dixon op cit
13 Fraser Rebecca, A history of Britain. London Chatto and Windus 2003 p760

Dixon - Fawcett Family associated with the firm

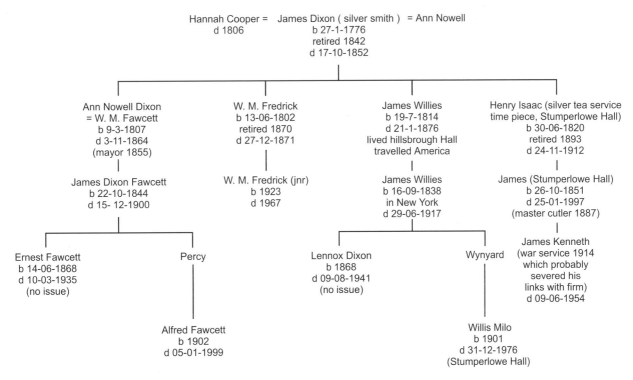

Note
Percy Fawcett and Wynyard Dixon never worked for the firm. Their sons were the last generations of management

Electroplated Nickel Silver, etc.

Electroplating shop

EPNS is a technique by which silver is deposited on a base metal using an electric current. The process was patented in 1840 and is still used as the usual way of plating today. The base metal is an alloy based on copper, nickel and zinc and I understand it is usually called nickel silver though actually it contains no silver! However silver is deposited onto this base in order to produce the electroplated nickel silver. In recent times this has been the usual combination and process for making flatware and many household metal goods. Other alloys can be electroplated and other metals can be coated. Stainless steel cutlery can be silver-plated and goods can be plated with gold.

At Dixon's' 'EPNS' was a substantial part of the business for flatware (forks and spoon) in particular but also for hollow-ware such as trays, meat dishes, tea sets, cruet sets and fish knives. Products could be cast in one piece and production runs were fast and flexible.

Controversy exists as to who was the inventor of the process, which was claimed by Sheffield's Walker and Hall though Birmingham's Elkington and Co also had strong claims. (1) Looking back it would seem to be difficult to come to any certain conclusion but Geoffrey Tweedale (2) points out that several individuals were involved and that numerous patents were registered and improvements made to the original ideas. Winning the battle over who invented the process it was thought would add prestige to both the city and the manufacturer credited with the invention.

The process certainly enabled those manufacturers like Dixon's who took it up, to produce good quality products which were something of a halfway house between the cheaper Britannia metal products and those made from Sterling silver.

The first trade directory that I have found in which Dixon's' has an entry is Baines (1822) which cites Dixon and Smith as manufacturers of Britannia metal goods and dealers in cutlery etc. and gives their address as '16 Silver Street, proprietors of Rolling Mill, Green Lane'. (3)

A correspondent asked Milo Dixon in a letter in 1971 what the composition of Britannia metal was and his reply was that it was 95% tin, 4% antimony and 1% copper (4). As a metal it is similar to pewter another tin-based alloy. BM has a little more antimony in it and this makes it harder and therefore more suited to the processes of stamping and spinning. There is in Pawson and Brailsford an account of how it was made in 1862 (5): *The tin is melted and raised to a red heat in a cast iron trough. Into the liquid metal is poured the regulus of antimony, the copper and brass each of these having been reduced to a melted state. While they are poured in the compound is carefully stirred by the workman who has the management of it. When they are thoroughly mixed the compound is poured either to iron boxes, in which it cools in the shape of slabs, or into moulds in which it takes the form of ingots.... .It is sometimes called 'Princes metal' and is commonly styled by the workman 'white metal'.* It does look at lot like silver so much so that it was necessary to inscribe it as Britannia metal to avoid confusion with silverware. In a trade directory of 1825 Dixon and Son (late Dixon and Smith) are described as 'manufacturers of Britannia metal goods, spoons, tin, petty pans, scallop shells etc.' and are now based in Cornish Place. (6)

Fused Plate or old Sheffield Plate is frequently confused with EPNS. It is however a much older discovery and is a plating by fusion rather than by electrolysis. The person almost certainly responsible for this process was Thomas Boulsover who made a mistake in 1743 whilst repairing the handle of a knife by slightly

overheating the decorative knife handle so that the copper and silver fused together. One wonders what his 'customer' felt about the accident! However the experience started Thomas off on further experiments which led to the discovery that copper and silver fused together could be rolled to a desired size and thickness and still keep the same proportions of the two metals. The fused metal sheet could then be modelled into a required product. The silver was about a tenth of the thickness of the copper. One Sheffielder described it thus, "T'copper were as thick as t' missus cuts t' bread an' t' silver as thin as she spreads t' butter" (7) For more details of this process see Hatfield (8)
The technique was used mostly from the mid eighteenth to the mid nineteenth century and it was less a part of the recognised processes of Dixon's (founded in 1805) than working with Britannia metal or later the use of EPNS. However in the earlier section on Dixon's I noted that the 'old workman' said that in the early days Dixon's' had made buckles and it is possible that these were made from fused plate in the same way as Boulsover had, at one time, made buttons.

Sterling silver products were a substantial part of the Dixon output. Sterling silver is yet another alloy but contains at least 92.5% pure silver. Since 1975 silver goods above the weight of 7.78grams must be hallmarked to denote the purity of the precious metal. Since the middle ages some kind of marking system has been the rule in order to protect the purchaser. Sterling silver was used at Dixons more usually for the production of more prestigious goods that were to commemorate events both public and private. Silver teaspoons and cups for christening presents, trowels for laying foundation stones, all kinds of trophies for sports events and communion sets for churches were in the literature and could be made of sterling silver.

In the years following the First World War a product invented at another Sheffield firm became very important in the development of the table cutlery industry. A man called Harry Brierley (9) working in the Brown Firth research laboratories in 1913 discovered that low carbon steels containing only 12% chromium had the ability to resist corrosion. He was working on gun barrels but immediately saw the potential for cutlery. W.H. Hatfield developed the 'staybrite' brand of corrosion resistant steel in 1923 which had in it 18% chromium and 8% nickel. By 1934 at the Daily Mail Ideal Homes Exhibition, a wide variety of goods were being manufactured in this metal, letter boxes, cake stands, fish-fryers. The Second World War held up the development of domestic products but a photograph exhists of a display of cutlery, surgical instruments and kitchen implements in the research section of Firth Browns which predates the Sheffield blitz in 1942. There is no doubt that Dixon's were either producing goods made from this steel or experimenting with it in the 1920's. (See section on 'Marks, assay and trade') Some employees however felt the firm was too slow to adopt the new metal. It is difficult to know too much if this is the wisdom of hindsight or whether they were really ahead of the management of the time.

Undoubtedly the Dixon staple metal EPNS was a wonderful substitute for silver. It is exceedingly difficult to differentiate unless you are an expert and was a real asset to the Victorian middle classes who were wanting to acquire fashionable goods for the home and particularly for the dining room but who could not afford sterling silver. This was why Christopher Dresser felt it was important to produce his work in EPNS rather than silver (see chapter on Quality Pieces). He once wrote: *If the designer forms works which are expensive, he places them beyond the reach of those who might otherwise enjoy them(10).*

Sources
1 Tweedale Geoffrey, The Electro-Plate Controversy in *Aspects of Sheffield 1*, Ed. Melvin Jones Pub. Wharncliffe Publishing 1997 pp132-152.
2 Ibid
3 Baines Vol. 1 History and Directory of Yorkshire West Riding 1822
4 Sheffield Archives, Dixons' B447 Papers of Milo Dixon 1962-75 incl. Memoranda book 1962-75.
5 Pawson and Brailsford Illustrated Guide to Sheffield, this edition S.R. publishers 1971, p.168
6 Directory of Sheffield 1825 compiled by R.Gell p.33
7 Hatfield John and Julia The Oldest Sheffield Plater, 1974, The Advertiser Press ltd page 84
8 Ibid
9 See Hamilton Catherine, Firth Brown, A Sheffield Steel Company, 2000 Tempus Publishing pp 67ff
10 Quoted in de Castres Elizabeth, a guide to collecting silver, publication in association with J Goddard & sons Ltd 1980 p.76

TRADE MARK

Fishing Club

Alfred Fawcett, family director presents Fishing Trophy to Harry Cooper, 1972

Lindley, Baxter and Buxton and altogether a membership of about 80 men. By 1880 membership had levelled off to about 40 men and for several years this number was fairly consistent.

Amongst the founder members are my great grandfather Henry Cooper who was also a committee member. He, his three sons and two grandsons and one great grandson were all in successive years to be not only members but also winners of the annual trophy. If you won it 3 years in succession you got to keep it. The photograph shows Harry, Barrie's father and my uncle receiving the trophy from Mr Fawcett, one of the directors in the 1970's. It was Barrie who stopped Harry's third successive victory one year but Barrie also has a trophy like my teapot trophy that his father won in earlier years.

Teapot - Fishing Club prize won by my grandfather Henry Cooper 1930's

One of my earliest memories when visiting my Grandmother was of a 'silver' teapot. This I was told had been won as a fishing prize by my grandfather when he worked at Dixon's. He died of cancer a couple of months before I was born in 1942 but I understand that fishing was an important part of his life and he must therefore have won the trophy just before the second world war. The trophy has on it the Dixon's mark and is obviously EPNS (electro-plated nickel silver). It passed to my mother and when she died to me. It sits in our dining room.

Many years later I was to discover that Barrie had the original minute book of the firm's Fishing Club. This lists all the founder members and the rules of the fishing matches that were held annually. The book is an ordinary exercise book with the names recorded down the left hand column in copperplate handwriting and then columns ruled to record the payment of 'subs' each month. All the names are there, Cooper,

The annual subscription in the early years seems to have been substantial relative to the weekly wage. It was around 10/- a year and some paid monthly and others quarterly, annually or possibly simply when they were 'in funds'. Some of the directors, notably Alfred Fawcett, fished in competitions on behalf of the firm. Harry used to tell the story of being driven by Mr Fawcett in his Cooper Bristol car and being frightened out of his wits by the speed of the 'take off' never mind the speed of the journey. Mr Fawcett was well known for his sports cars and was a leading member of the Bugatti club.

The book records details of some of the early

Sorting out the prizes, early 1970's
Left to right: Harry Cooper, Andrew Andrews
and Colin Baxter

Few results are recorded in those early days but I note that in 1884 great grandfather was 3rd. Harry won this competition 14 times and Barrie 3 times.

I am surprised at the distances that they travelled for the match. I recognise that the local rivers were probably by this time too polluted to support fish however in a previous era salmon actually lived in the Don. Barrie can remember around the time he started as an apprentice hearing stories from one of the older workman, Tommy Middleton, of how years ago he used to throw the remainder of his sandwiches from the canteen veranda to the salmon in the Don. Apparently there was a spot further up called 'salmon pastures'. Family tradition claims that defective spoons and forks were simply thrown out of the window straight into the river that flowed very close to Cornish Place. If this were general practice along the Don it would by the 1880's contain few fish let alone salmon.

committee meetings including the rules that were drawn up for the first competitions. These included

- That one hour be allowed for refreshments
- That no member be allowed to fish before the match; any member found so doing will be disqualified
- That no member be allowed to go to his place until he has been searched by the constable, or who may be appointed. Any member found with fish in his possession will be disqualified.

In 1885 the club fished at Appleby near Brigg and on the 30th July 1887 at Crowle both in Lincolnshire. These were excursions by rail travel. In the accounts for 1881 there is an entry for 41 railway tickets which cost the princely sum of £5/2/6d. During this period the largest amount of expenditure was actually on the prizes which in 1882 were a dinner service which

Fishing Club subscriptions 1875, No 82 is Silver Stamper Henry Cooper

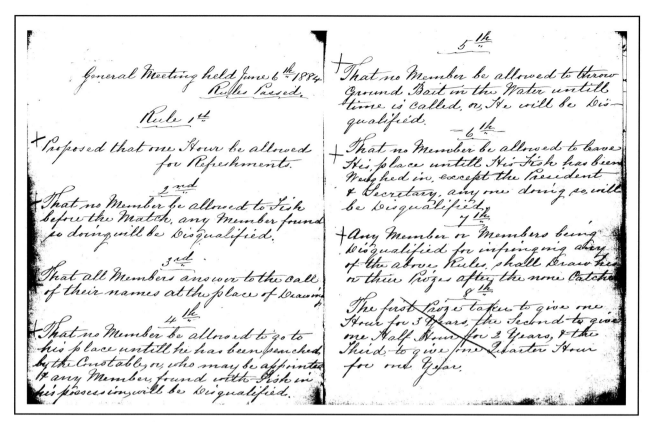

Fishing Club Rules, June 1884

cost £11 and two tea services which cost £2.5/-. On August 4th they lashed out and had 40 suppers for £5. In later years the matches were usually at Lincolnshire South Forty Foot near Boston and they travelled by coach. It became a tradition on the way home to stop in Worksop where they all had a drink.

Records are sparse until the 1950's by which time there was an established annual match against George Clark's Rolling Mills. Each firm put out a team. The size varied each year though obviously each firm fielded the same number of fishermen and on occasions Dixon's lent the other side fishermen though I have it on good authority that Dixon's had first pick. The winners were decided by totalling up the weight of all fish caught by all participants. I am pleased to record that in most years between 1949 and 1967 Dixon's were clear winners and on 10 occasions one of the Cooper clan was in first place. In most years Mr. Fawcett was usually about half way down the list with his contribution to the total weight of fish caught.

I also understand from Barrie that they had competitions called odds and evens. They drew for odds or evens to form a pair and fished one against the other for 2/6d.

The club survived almost until the end and in 1975 had its centenary. All the members of the committee received a small 'silver' fish as a memento (see photograph). Harry's is still in the possession of the family.

Sources
Originals held by author

Silver fish presented to members of the Fishing Club Committee on its centenary, 1975

TRADE MARK

Guns and Other Sporting Paraphernalia

Milo Dixon in shooting gear

Fishing was I believe the nearest any of my family came to country sports. As can be seen from the photograph of Milo Dixon, the Fawcetts and Dixons were enthusiastic sportsmen. They held around 1900 the lease for the shooting rights on Unstone Moor.(1) So I assume Milo was following a family tradition.Alfred Fawcett, a family director in the middle part of the twentieth century was a keen fly fisherman as well as being a member of the firm's fishing club. Shooting as a sport was however a huge market for Dixon's products. In a Sheffield Trade Directory of 1834 (2) it is recorded amongst other things Dixon's manufactured 'copper powder flasks, shot belts etc'. Around 1840 Dixon's bought out the firm of Mr Batty a powder flask manufacturer and his range of products was added to that of their own.

According to an article in 'The Journal of the Arms and Armour Society (3) the writer had seen a manuscript description books covering 1848-1902. In 1848 listed products included cap primers, chargers, dog calls, magazines, oil bottles, powder flasks, pistol flasks, shot pouches, shot belts, straps, flask and pouch tops and their accompanying levers and springs. In the catalogue of 1883, the products are described as a 'range of goods produced by one of world's leading manufacturers of shooting accessories'.

The Pawson and Brailsford original Guide to Sheffield was written in 1862 (4). In the guide it is claimed *'Messrs. Dixon and Sons, of Sheffield, are a hundred to one against the world,' says Frank Forrester, the author of 'Field Sports in the United States'*

Hawksley's and Muzzles

By 1861 there were 35 new cartridge implements such as re-cappers, fillers, cutter scissors, closers, carriers and cartridge hooks. In 1883 they had produced a 58-page catalogue, the whole of which is reproduced in the above quoted Journal. The range was considerably reduced by 1915 when only 10 powder flasks were available. These were made from old dies 8 of which were originally Hawksley and 2 of Dixon's and these were for a short time revived in 1957 for the US market. Hawksley's had been taken over by Dixon's in April 1947and separate accounts were kept until 1954 when the annual turn over was stable at around £16,000 and the wage bill about £4600. It was then merged with Dixon's own powder flask department.

Milo Dixon(5) recorded in 1969 that some years previously they had bought up 'Muzzles' who were loading implement makers. Apparently when breach loading guns came into general use Dixon's started to make individual loading implements. In this field there was innovation. Mr Simpson in the department perfected the 'climax' loading machine. This is described in the 1908-11 catalogue as 'the only machines offered to the trade that block automatically when the cartridge cases are loaded; they are the only machines which can be guaranteed not to cut

TRADE MARK

Powder flasks, made for American market

the shot in working; they excel all other machines of the kind for simplicity of adjustment and accuracy of measurement'.

Hawkbird Killer
In 1887 Dixon's entered into an agreement (6) with a William Moffatt of Gateshead, County Durham who was an ironmonger who had obtained a patent for his invention known as the 'combined hawkbird killer' for killing wounded birds. He appointed 'the said firm sole manufacturers and wholesale agents thereof for Great Britain and Ireland for 7 years commencing 1st November.' The firm agreed to pay a royalty and to number each one consecutively.

Sporting equipment was in the earlier years a substantial part of the business. In 1864 there were 53 employees in this department out of a total workforce of 424 work people. (7) In the 1908-11 catalogue there are on offer such luxuries as hunting canteens, saddle flasks, deer stalking or second-horseman's canteens (what is a second-horseman?!), hunting knives, sporting and champagne knives (interesting combination), a huge variety of breech-loading implements not to mention cartridge closers, loaders and extractors.

Dixon's stopped making many of these products around 1953 because of a shortage of labour though in the 1950's they had as previously started to make powder flasks for the US market and large quantities were still sold in 1969. (8)

The war effort
The fact that they were in this line of business enabled them to contribute to the war effort in both world wars. In June 1916 they were granted a licence to sell parts of firearms under the 'Defense of the Realm (consolidation) regulations'. The firm made significant contributions to the production of arms. It is recorded in the report of the Victory celebrations that during this period the factory was adapted and they manufactured 1,000,000 steel helmets, 100,000 of pairs of piston rings for aeroplane engines, 250,000 liquid gas shells and many thousands of parts for mine and depth charges. (8)

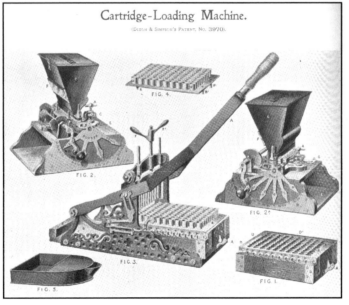

Cartridge-Loading Machine.
(DIXON & SIMPSON'S PATENT, No. 3970).

In Mr Constantine's notes (9) there is in September 1938 a rare reference to the political situation. He writes: *at this point everything points to us being called upon to assist France in repelling the German Army who were intent upon seizing by force certain territory in Czechoslovakia...*

In March, the Steel firm Hadfields asked if Dixon's would press steel helmets. Mr Constantine writes that Dixon's gave them an assurance that Dixon's would press from their steel (to be supplied free) helmets of the usual war office type provided that they (Hadfields) received an order. The war office had requested the name of the firm to whom the pressing would be entrusted. It seems that in the first year they expected to be able to press 436,000 requiring the employment of 10 skilled men, 10 unskilled and 6 women.

By September 1938 the pressing had been checked with current drawings and found to be generally satisfactory to dimensions and weight. However, Mr Constantine reports that, *exception is taken to size of holes which are found to be too large in diameter and to bulges and bumps which occur when radius of brim and the radius of the dome merge*. The price per 143/4 square of steel was 2/6d(7). It is possible that the press displayed as a feature in Cornish Place to day(see chapter on industrial buildings) was used for pressing out helmets in the war.

The Collectors' Market.

I found an undated newspaper cutting in the archives in the work's dairy (10) which claimed that American servicemen in WW2 used to call at the firm who sold them the few old powder flasks still in stock which the Americans took home as prized antiques. Apparently the word spread and even in 1959-60 the firm was selling about 1000 of these powder flasks every year specifically for the American market. Originally they were for the muzzle loading of Colt firearms and for the hand filling of metal cartridge cases which, after being fired were whenever possible collected and used again. Presumably these had been used extensively in the days of the wild west.

I knew a lot about Dixon's as a child from various family stories though I never recall hearing anything about this aspect of their trade. Nevertheless I think it possible that my great great grandfather's youngest brother John Cooper did work in this department of Dixon's as he is recorded on the census of 1851 as a powder flask maker.

Sources

1 Sheffield Archives, Dixon's A284 lease of shooting rights, Unstone
2 Pigot and Co. National Commercial Directory Sheffield section (Column46)
3 The Journal of the Arms and Armour Society Vol V, No 3 Sept 1965
4 Pawson and Brailsford Illustrated Guide to Sheffield, this edition S.R. publishers 1971, p.170
5 Sheffield Archives Dixon's B447 Papers of Milo Dixon c1862-75 incl memoranda book 1962-73
6 Sheffield Archives Dixon's A295 Draft agreement Moffatt and Dixon Hawkbird killer 1887
7 Sheffield Archives, Dixon's A250 Wages paid by Ms. James Dixon & Sons to the workpeople in their employ for the week ending March 11th 1864.

8 Magazine, The watchmaker, jeweller, silversmith and optician July 1919, *James Dixon and Sons, Sheffield, in war and peace.*
9 Sheffield Archives, Dixon's A188 Volume marked S.Constantine, random notes of some interest 1936-39
10 Sheffield Archives, Dixon's A195 Volume marked 'Cash Book', but containing memoranda and notes 1952-62'

Deer-Stalking or Second-Horseman's Canteens

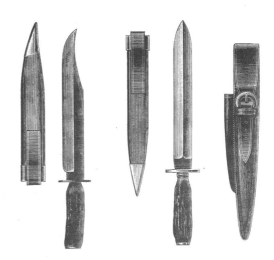

Hunting Knives

TRADE MARK

29

Hillsborough

Naming the roads

I was born and lived until my mid teens in Dorothy Rd, Hillsborough, Sheffield 6. I always thought Dorothy, a girl's name, a bit odd for the name of a road. Running parallel was a Garry Rd and I thought Garry was a boy's name. According to Peter Harvey(1) it was the name of a Dixon family pet and the name of the road having been changed in 1903 from Garth to Garry. I later realised that the road at right angles, Dixon Rd, was named after the Dixon family and that the roads that joined it or crossed it were all named after members of the family. Dorothy was born in 1897 and was a V.A.D. in Egypt in the First World War. There was also a Lennox, Willis and Wynyard Rd. These as a child, I didn't recognise as people's first names. Wynyard was, I understand, a noted game shot and was by profession a surveyor. Peter Perry recalls having to empty a room at Cornish Place that was full of Wynyard's plans for the Dixon Road area. He assumed they had been moved there when Wynyard died. They were simply burned! Lennox went into the family firm and Willis was a family name that was given to several of the boys in different generations. It was only later that I realised that the Dixon in Dixon Rd was the same Dixon's as the firm for whom my grandfather and uncles and generations before them and after them had all worked.

Other roads built around the same time were given the family names of some of the people the Dixon women married. These included Shepperson and Fielding. Florence Dixon married Sir Charles William Fielding in 1899. He owned land in Sussex and during World War 1 he was Director General of Food production. He later wrote about the problems faced by British Farmers from imported Commonwealth food. My great grandfather either purchased or had houses built in Fielding Rd. Two of his daughters, my great aunts, lived in this road with their families and inherited the houses when he and his wife both died in 1928. Warner Rd also has a Dixon link. Sir Pelham (Plum) Warner (1873-1963) was at Rugby School with both Archibald and Lennox Dixon and they were close friends. He was onetime England and Middlesex Cricket captain and later president of the MCC.

Hillsborough Hall

Hillsborough Hall

I was later to discover that Hillsborough Library to which I was as a child, a frequent visitor had been the home of one of the James Dixons. Hillsborough Hall must have been a lovely old house. It was built in 1779 as a tribute to Lord Downshire who lived in Hillsborough, Downshire in Northern Ireland. Its' first owner was a great admirer of Lord Downshire. It stood and the library as it is to-day, still stands in an area of parkland which at the beginning of the twentieth century became one of the city parks. Two generations of the family lived at Hillsborough Hall, James Willis born in 1814 and who died in 1876 and his eldest son, also James Willis who was born in 1838 in New York and who died in 1917. It was eventually bought by Sheffield Corporation.

There are numerous papers relating to this Hillsborough Hall and Estate auction in Sheffield Archives. The estate seemed to be broken up into lots and Wynyard Dixon as the estate agent and surveyor handled the task of dividing the estate into 'lots'. Amongst the papers are a variety of maps and plans one of which shows a group of cottages called Dixon's cottages on Leppings Lane. (2)These could have been tithe cottages for estate workers or servants. The whole process seems to have gone on for years. There is a letter written by Wynyard in 1916 which demonstrates what an apt name for the suburb 'Hillsborough' is, as I once thought like many other people that it was named as a response to the hilly nature of the topography!

The land to the topside of Dixon Road adjoining Mr Taylor's house was so high above the road that I could not get any builder to take it. I arranged with Mr Thomas Booth that if he would take a good slice of the land I would pay him £20 towards the extra expense in building on the high land. He has now built 4 houses and the enclosed account according to the agreement should now be paid.

It also seems likely that the Dixon's were in some way responsible for the 'Horse and Jockey Public House' as there is a vast amount of correspondence re the liquor licence in the same set of papers.

I imagine in the James Dixons' time it was all parkland with trees and the lake and surrounded by fields. Lord Roy Hattersley (3) an ex deputy leader of the Labour Party lived in this locality as a boy and describes making considerable use of Hillsborough Park and the library 10 years or so before I did. He writes:

When we detoured down Dorothy Road to catch the tram at one stop nearer to the city centre than the Middlewood terminus, we thought of the lucky young ladies who had been brought up in the library at Hillsborough Park. It had become a classic northern civic amenity. Part of it-simply to amaze and delight all who beheld its' beauties-was immaculate acres into which careful flower beds had been cut. The rest intended for private recreation-tennis, rowing, bowls played with eccentric precision on the gently convex 'crown' and kicking balls about on the vast expanse of bare brown soil where athletic feet had worn the grass away. We approached the library from the ornamental end of the park.....At first my mother accompanied me into the 'junior section' and selected my books with a ruthless disregard of my own preferences.

Interestingly Roy's mother was to become a Lord Mayor of the City of Sheffield as did at least one member of the Dixon-Fawcett family. Enid Hattersley was definitely 'old labour' and lived in the same house in Hillsborough almost until her death around the turn of the Millenium when she was around 100 years old.

Wadsley Church, Sheffield Wednesday, Wadsley Hall

Hillsborough Park was usually the scene of the 'Whit walks' for local Sunday Schools when I was

Wadsley Church

a child. I understand that in earlier days it was the venue for the Whitsuntide treat for the scholars of Wadsley Parish Church. The Dixon's always presented the children on these occasions with a bun, an orange and a new penny. In the church on the wall up by the altar is a plaque in memory of James and Ann Dixon, the first generation of Dixon's to live at Hillsborough Hall. James for many years paid the fire insurance premuim for the church which had been built in 1834. On Easter Day 1884 the church roof caught fire. The villagers tried to control the fire with buckets of water. Eventually the horse drawn fire engine arrived. Although the roof fell into the church, the action of the firemen in turning the jets on the heated, blackened timbers prevented further destruction. Within days a restoration committee was formed. Amongst it's members were James Willis Dixon, Fredrick Fowler and Sir John Fowler, both engineers.

The insurance covered a substantial amount of the restoration costs and other generous offers came from various families including the Dixons and Fowlers. The church re-opened fully restored in February 1885, the Dixons entertained to lunch the Archbishop of York prior to the re-opening service held at 3pm.

When it rained rather than going to the park on Whit walks my generation went to Owlerton to Sheffield Wednesday's Football Ground. This is very close to the park. The Dixon's had also had a hand in providing Sheffield Wednesday's ground. The Midland Railway Company took over their original ground at Olive Grove. They made several attempts to buy land for a ground and were saved by Mr J.W. Dixon of Hillsborough Hall who made them a proposition of a 10 acre site at Owlerton. The first match was played in September 1899 and they beat Chesterfield 5-1

TRADE MARK

in a Division 2 game. It was a golden era as they went on to win the Division 1 championship in 1903 and 1904 and the F.A. cup in 1907. (5)

Two noises stick in my mind from my childhood in the 1950's in Hillsborough: the roar when Sheffield Wednesday scored on Saturday afternoons, (more frequently I recall, than in the modern era) and the relentless thud, thud, thud in the distance of what I think now was a tilt hammer though I am not sure where exactly that would have been located.

Neepsend Bridgre

The Coopers were obviously linked to the Dixon's because so many Coopers were in the silver trade but Henry Cooper, my grandfather married Florence Emily Bailey and that family also lived very close to Hillsborough Hall. The Bailey's lived in Burrowlea Rd and Park View which looks on to Hillsborough Park. My great grandmother Annie Bailey was by birth a Froggatt and her father was a gardener and general servant. I wonder whether he worked at Hillsborough Hall?

Running along the top of Lennox, Dorothy and Garry Rd is Far Lane. Wadsley Hall which is situated on Far Lane also has a Dixon link. Going even further back to the 1700's one of the Dixon family Hannah, married a Sam Fowler of Wadsley from whom are descended Sir John Fowler and Fredrick Fowler, the engineers. Sir John lived at Wadsley Hall and was the engineer responsible for the building of the Forth Bridge.

Neepsend Bridge

Neepsend adjoins the Hillsborough, Owlerton area and in 1856 William Fredrick Dixon led an initiative to get the local council to build a bridge across the River Don at Neepsend. William Fredrick along with William Butcher, John Green and George Hounsfield paid £1000 into the Bridge Account. The Sheffield Independent of February 16th 1856 reported council proceedings in which the majority of the Council seemed to be arguing that no bridge could be built until the landowners had built the approach roads on both sides. William Fredrick continued to press them to fulfil the agreement an original copy of which is in the archives (5). It states that 'the mayor, alderman and burgesses shall and will at their own expense on and before

the thirty first day of December 1855 construct so as to be ready and fit for public use the said Neepsend bridge of the width of 40 feet as aforesaid and approaches there to from Neepsend Lane and Penistone Rd respectively in the course shown on the plan here unto annexed' There does not seem in that much room for argument! It was built shortly after this and as a stone built structure survived the ravages of the 1864 flood.

Without a doubt, the Dixon's made a huge difference to the development of Hillsborough as indeed they did to the City. Members of the family held various civic offices including Master Cutler. Lennox and his nephew Milo were both to become guardians of the Assay office. Cornish Place where the firm was based until its' closure is also in Sheffield 6 though about 3 miles nearer to the City Centre.

Sources
1. Harvey Peter. Street names of Sheffield, Sheaf Publishing 1991
2. Sheffield Archives, Dixon's series B 440 Miscellaneous papers J W Dixon relating to his estate
3. Hattersley Roy, Yorkshire Boyhood, Chatto and Windus 1983. p.81
4. Joe Castle, Wadsley Church in Victorian Times - pamphlet printed by Bentley Press.
5. Banks W. Football, pub. in 'Hillsborough by her people'. Ed. Dr Helen Mattas privately published by the local history society about 1983. p.38
6. Sheffield Archives, Dixon's A297 Neepsend Bridge.

Industrial Buildings

Dixon's from Ball Bridge, looking upstream

Victorian splendour

The factory buildings that appeared during the Industrial revolution are in external appearance very often magnificent. They seem to me to be temples and symbols of wealth creation for those who built and owned them. Making this point there is, more or less next door to what was the Dixon's factory, Green Lane Works. This building today has a gateway with a central arch that carries the name of the works and on either side of the arch are sculptured panels of figures representing 'Vulcan' and 'Art'. Originally in the pediment stood the royal coat of arms surrounded by draped flags, though these were destroyed in an air raid during the Second World War. Conditions for the workers on the inside of the factory however rarely reflected the outer splendour.

The view of Dixon's Cornish Place from the nearby Ball Bridge over the River Don is an example of this kind of building and though not quite as splendid as the Green Lane Works is still a handsome monument to its era. In fact in the 1820's the building of Ibbotson's Globe works on Penistone Rd and developments there in the next twenty to thirty years obscured the Cornish Place entrance to Dixon's. It was deemed necessary therefore to build a new façade worthy of the firm and to advertise its existence.

Modern development

This area around Kelham Island Industrial Museum has since 1984 been designated an Industrial Conservation area. This beautiful solid red brick building that was for over 150 years Dixon's silversmiths has since the late 1990's housed luxury apartments and offices on the banks of the Don. Many of these apartments contain features that are original pieces of Dixon machinery. The building is preserved and restored with its attractive round-topped windows. According to the developer's publicity material, *original brick and stone staircases and balastrades have been renovated, 700 sash windows repaired and 200 replaced with replicas of the originals and over half the internal walls shotblasted to expose the feature brickwork.* (1)

TRADE MARK

Looking downstream, towards Ball Bridge

Before and after the flood

Ball Bridge dates back to the 1860's and was built to replace the earlier footbridge destroyed by the rushing water of the 1864 Sheffield Flood. It lay just below the weir for a long time twisted like a wood shaving. The building stood firm though the foundations on the riverside had to be rebuilt to a depth of 12 feet. In addition, the floodwater did considerable damage to dies and stamps in the lower rooms. There was also some damage to the rolling mills, gas pipes had to be cleared and reset, steps in the stable yard needed repairing and cleaning as did some of the doors and stonework. Large quantities of raw materials were also rendered useless (2). There is also a contemporary description of an old clerk called Thorpe who lived on the premises possibly as some kind of caretaker/night watchman. The flood washed him in the direction of the wooden gates and he was banged against these 3 times but they held and he was able to cling on to them and thus avoid being swept away by the torrent. (3).

Until the mid 1700's the site was part of the open fields along the side of the Don. Clayton Dam field covered an area of just under 4000 square yards. Dixon's began aptly enough in Silver Street but in 1819 a rolling mill on what had been part of Clayton Field was conveyed to the partnership of Dixon and Smith. This was the beginning of the Cornish Place era. Silver and plated goods were made on the site from at least 1830 when Dixon acquired the firm of Nicholson, Ashforth and Cutts.

Following the formalised co-partnership agreement between James Dixon, William Fredrick Dixon, James Willis Dixon and William Fawcett in 1836, the firm took over land and buildings to the south of the original site and new workshops were constructed. During the

1840's and 50's the firm consolidated and large parts of Cornish Place next to Ball Street and Green Lane were rebuilt. The building programme continued into the 1860's with the building of the large six and seven storey ranges fronting Ball Street and the River Don. Modifications were made in the 1870's and the boiler house was rebuilt in the 1880's. The first major new building was in the 1890's and this was to be followed in the early part of the 20th century by the refurbishment of existing buildings when the workforce numbered 900 people.

By the 1920's stainless steel was increasingly used throughout the industry to make both flatware and hollow-ware and silver and silver-plated goods declined in quantity.

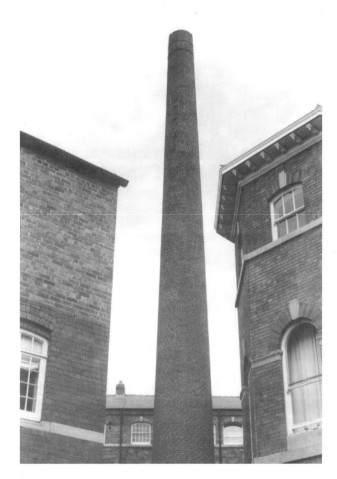

The chimney and other upgrading

In 1900 most of the machinery still ran off line shafting which was directly powered from the steam engine in the engine house. I assume the chimney (still in place to-day) was a part of this building. There is a reference in the archives to the chimney being 45 yards high and that it was repointed in 1898 to about half way up costing £66. (4). The same source reports that in 1937

A series of photographs by H G Penfold taken in early 1990 as Dixons nears the end and awaits the developers

Through the big door was a bust of James Dixon at the bottom of the main staircase (see chapter on James Dixon)

TRADE MARK

35

Rough Guide to Dixon's in the 1950's as recalled by Barrie Cooper

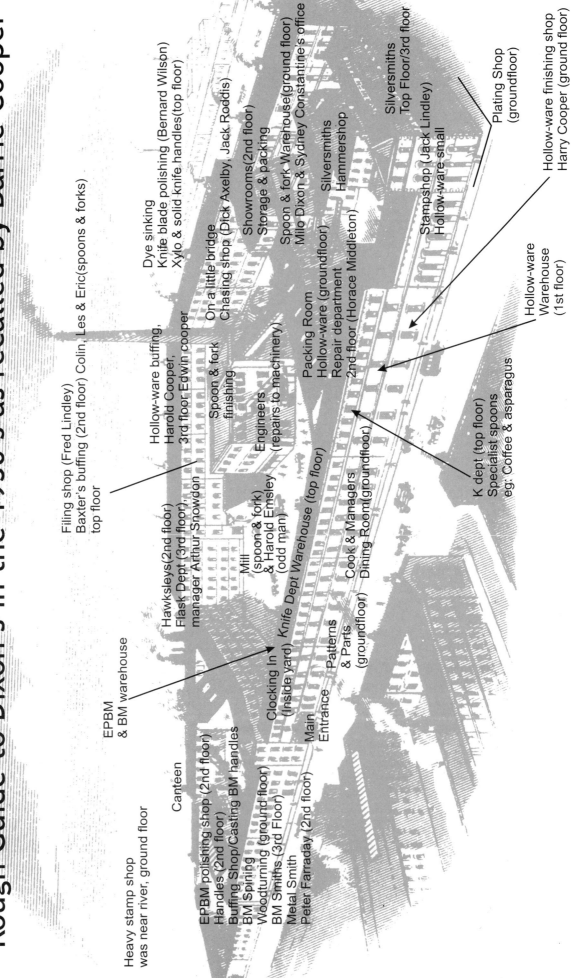

Heavy stamp shop
was near river, ground floor

Canteen

EPBM
& BM warehouse

EPBM polishing shop (2nd floor)
Handles (2nd floor)
Buffing Shop/Casting BM handles
BM Spining
Woodturning (ground floor)
BM Smiths (3rd Floor)
Metal Smith
Peter Farraday (2nd floor)

Filing shop (Fred Lindley)
Baxter's buffing (2nd floor) Colin, Les & Eric(spoons & forks)
top floor

Hollow-ware buffing,
Harold Cooper,
3rd floor Edwin cooper

Hawksleys(2nd floor)
Flask Dept (3rd floor),
manager Arthur Snowdon

Spoon & fork
finishing

Mill
(spoon & fork)
& Harold Emsley
(odd man)

Clocking In
(Inside yard)

Knife Dept Warehouse (top floor)

Main
Entrance

Patterns
& Parts
(groundfloor)

Cook & Managers
Dining Room(groundfloor)

Dye sinking
Knife blade polishing (Bernard Wilson)
Xylo & solid knife handles(top floor)

On a little bridge
Chasing shop (Dick Axelby, Jack Roddis)

Showrooms(2nd floor)
Storage & packing

Spoon & fork Warehouse(ground floor)
Milo Dixon & Sydney Constantine's office

Silversmiths
Hammershop

Packing Room
Hollow-ware (groundfloor)
Repair department
2nd floor (Horace Middleton)

Engineers
(repairs to machinery)

Silversmiths
Top Floor/3rd floor

Stampshop (Jack Lindley)
Hollow-ware small

Plating Shop
(groundfloor)

Hollow-ware finishing shop
Harry Cooper (ground floor)

Hollow-ware
Warehouse
(1st floor)

K dept (top floor)
Specialist spoons
eg: Coffee & asparagus

W. Tomlinson of Leeds quoted £65 for repairing the canopy and repointing all round the total length. This quote was accepted and the work was completed in January 1937. It is recorded in 1961 that one of the bands on the boiler chimney crashed down on to the glass roof of the spoon and fork finishing shop. No-one was injured but there was a lot of damage. Peter Perry as a young man was working under this glass roof when this event occurred. He says it was terrifying and he ran out of the building. Not only were they showered with glass but overhead electricity cables were caught by falling debris and sparks were shooting everywhere. From this time onwards the chimney looked as it does in the photograph. In earlier drawings like the one on the opposite page, it had a kind of band round the top. It was stated that one band had been replaced in 1960 and that the firm concerned had not reported that the other band was in any state of disrepair (5). In 1969 Milo Dixon recorded that the stonework and steel bands were badly corroded and that repairs and new bands cost £678 and additional work on the water- cooling system a further £175 (6).

In 1937 as a result of pressure from the factory inspector, a new lift was installed by Wadsworth and Co of Bolton through Robert Neill and Co. of Sheffield. The running costs were about one sixth of what it cost to run the old lift. The factory inspector in 1961 indicated the need for guards on presses and the need for fire escapes. He also suggested that an old iron staircase that was no longer used should be dismantled. Roger Tetley who worked at the firm in the 1950's remembers a woman getting what he thinks was a drill through her hand. A doctor came and gave her chloroform whilst she was extracted from the machine. Whether this could have been prevented with appropriate guards, who knows? Fred Lindley, a stamper, also lost an arm in an incident with the stamp machine.

Manufacturing Gas
It is possible that in about 1896 the company set up the facility to make gas from coal. In a notebook in the archives is a job description for a newly appointed gas maker (7) This is dated May 8th 1896 and includes the task of 'to stack the coal required for gas making so as to leave room to walk where required.' The job also included changing the retorts when necessary, keeping all the valves clean and in proper working order and pumping the siphons. Wages were 30/- a

Surviving press now incorporated into Cornish Place City Living

week and the conditions included the imposition of a 1/- fine if the factory was without gas. It seems that it was possible to turn off their own supply and switch to that of the local gas company. I am not sure whether in 1937 when Davy Bros installed a new boiler this was anything to do with the gas making or was something quite separate.

Some buildings pre first world war had early electrical systems mostly for lighting. During the war some line shafting was converted to electric power. Steam power continued to be used for the rolling mill and for many of the presses and hammers and it was sometime before modernisation allowed for the removal of all line shafting. The provision of toilets and washrooms came in the building phase following 1906. In March 1938 the possibility of a dust extraction plant was being considered for the EPNS hollow-ware shop. This it was recorded would require a space the size of one of the cellars under the hollow-ware finishing shop. One was finally installed in August 1947 in the spoon and fork finishing shop and was such a success one was immediately ordered for the hollow-ware shop. Throughout the 1960's and 70's government legislation and 'wear and tear' demanded a lot of expenditure on the buildings

TRADE MARK

and in June 1970 Milo Dixon recorded that a big fire destroyed the wages and accounts office, girls' staff toilets, 2 lamp shops and that the nearby bridge and stairs were unusable.

'Archus' Findings
The detailed analysis below is from a report produced in 2001 by 'Arcus' (8).

B1 Offices and workshops. Originally a 2 storey brick building with a third storey added in 1903. A timekeepers hut was added to the N.E. end in the late 19th century.

B2 S.E. end is shown in a 1828 engraving. First floor used as pattern making shops and possibly casting shop and general storage

B3 Workshop range

B4 Workshop with office above

B5 Stamp shop

B6&7 Workshop Block originally steam powered.

B8 Last and grandest of the mid nineteenth century improvements Built 1850's to accommodate showrooms and offices as well as extending the existing workshop space.

B9 New façade. The space below the second floor windows displayed the enamel sign of James Dixon and Sons. It was still in place in 1996 and was presumably removed by the developer Gleeson's.

B10 Plating shop built in 1850's

B11 Engine House and Boiler House extension.

B12 Offices, workshops and warehouses. Built in 1890 these buildings replaced an earlier building on the same alignment

B13 Workshops

B14 Garage and die sinking built prior to 1906

B15 Prior to 1906 was one storey; two more added after 1920

B16 Polishing shops and storage built just prior to First World War.

B17 Non ferrous crucible furnace built 1920-21 and located on the north and east walls. Part of building 2 was used for its' north and east walls and building 3 for the south wall. There was a brick built single room on the ground floor and a cellar below

B18 Timekeeper's cottage.

According to the Centenary brochure (9) the design of the works and the placing of the machinery was the result of a careful study and demonstrated a thorough understanding of the processes and the machinery required. Each workshop was placed so as to follow the order of the various processes of manufacture. As the century went on, corrosion resulting from air pollution, the weather and general wear and tear took a toll. In addition regulations following factory acts required upgrading and updating as health and safety issues were increasingly addressed. I think by the 1950's expenditure on the buildings was probably quite a drain on the firm at a time when trade was sluggish and investment was needed in new machinery.

There was also a failure to rationalise the building so that it efficiently housed a much smaller workforce. After the First World War the carefully planned layout for the workforce of 900 was increasingly irrelevant and by the 1950's time was wasted moving products around the different processes which were scattered around the large building.

Sources
1   Gleeson Publicity Leaflet. 1999
2   Sheffield Archives A330 Compensation Claims, Sheffield Flood ??
3   Sheffield Telegraph Aug 18th 1933 Reminiscences of James Dixon
4   Sheffield Archives, Dixon's A188 Volume marked S. Constantine random notes of some interest 1936-39.
5   Sheffield archives Dixon's A195. Volume marked 'Cash Book', but containing memoranda and notes 1952-62'
6   Sheffield Archives, Dixon's B447 Papers of Milo Dixon c.1962-73 incl. memoranda book.
7   Sheffield Archives Dixon's A192 Notebook containing extracts from documents, notes etc 1896-1923
8   Archaeological Building Recording at Cornish Place Sheffield February 2001 by Paul Belford. Archaeological Research and Consultancy, University of Sheffield School of Archaeology
9   Centenary Brochure 1906 p. 13-15

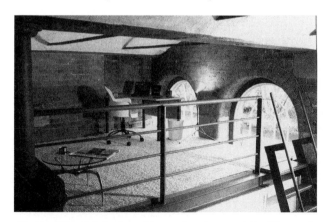
An apartment interior after redevelopment by Gleeson's

TRADE MARK

James Dixon, the Founder (1776-1852)

James Dixon the founder of the firm would today be described as an entrepreneur. He set up the firm with a Mr Smith in 1806 to manufacture goods made from Britannia metal, Sheffield Plate and pewter. The partnership lasted 16 years until Mr Smith retired from the firm and during this time the firm moved from its' original location in Silver Street to the place from which it became famous, Cornish Place. Charles Dixon suggests that he gave financial support to Mr. Smith's widow after the death of her husband. (1) According to the same source he had served an apprenticeship as an engraver.

The man

James Dixon was one of eleven children. He seems to have been an energetic man who was willing to embrace all the developing technology of the age to advance the production of goods in his chosen field. He was one of the first manufacturers to take up the use of steam power. There can be little doubt that he did put down the foundations of a business which was handed down through generations of the family and which at its' peak had a worldwide reputation for both quality and innovation. To some extent this success must have been due to vision, innovative and organisational skills as well as a capacity to get the best out of people. This must have been part of what the firm gained from its founder.

One of his early notebooks is still available (2). It is obvious from this notebook that he set a pattern discernable through the following generations that finding customers and keeping them satisfied was a priority for the top management. The notebook in essence is a simple record of all his customers in London, Birmingham and Wolverhampton. This being 1822 it is of course handwritten in copperplate handwriting and makes use for additional clarity of black and red ink. In black he records the name and address of the account holder and then in red ink details of the terms of the account which could be cash, money, to have an account of goods returned and packing cases, monthly credit, 2 monthly bill (he is allowed portuage). As an example we have VCT Rotton, Dorrington Street Clerkinwell £42/10 to pay cash in consequence of 2½% being taken off the net amount. There are a huge number of London contacts and his address in front of the book is 8 York Street, Covent Garden. All of this suggests a very well organised person, a negotiator willing to give different terms to different buyers and someone very willing to take the risks of travelling by stage coach from Sheffield to London or elsewhere and then of making his way around the Capital either on foot or in some horse drawn vehicle.

His own claims
On his seventieth birthday 4 years after his retirement in 1842 he claimed that when he started the business he was determined that nothing should go out of the factory bearing his name that should disgrace him and that this was the keynote to the reputation of the firm. His portrait hung in the works virtually until its closure and his bust stood in the main entrance until the building was closed for business. The bust is still with British Silver Ware at their offices in Heeley, Sheffield. He bought from the Heralds College in about 1849 a great coat of arms and became a gentleman by purchase. The motto was 'Fide et Constantia', 'Faith and Perseverance'. His roots were in the Ecclesfield area and an ancestor's marriage is recorded in the parish registers in 1619 and he is buried in Ecclesfield Churchyard as are a number of the Dixon family.

His contribution to Sheffield
He was a Sheffielder by birth and he was active in the process of enabling the city to obtain 'incorporation as a municipal borough'. It is said that he would have become Lord Mayor but that he offended the liberal party. (3) According to Mr James Willis Dixon in his speech at the centenary celebrations in 1906 James had been left no money by has father even though all his siblings had an equal share. He had said that *Jim could take care of himself, and left him nothing*. The speaker went on to say 'Jim did take care of himself, and he also took care of his servants, his workpeople and his children and the poor...He was also a great builder of house property. Besides building Silver Street Works and Cornish Place, he built Hanover Villa, Broom Lodge, Hanover Square, Birley House, Moscar Farm, Dixon Street and various other streets, a large school at Doncaster, chapels and public houses for where one is the other is sure to be not far away.'

He believed in the public welfare and supported and contributed to the Sheffield Infirmary which was situated only a mile or so from Cornish Place. It is always difficult to judge from this distance in time whether an employer was held in high regard by workers or whether gestures were motivated by less wholesome motives. However on James Dixon's 70th birthday, (four years after his retirement), he was presented by the workforce of 400 people with a silver epergne costing 200 guineas. There is a story that he was very moved by this gift and that he gave to each person as a 'thank-you' a gold sovereign. Like many of us, he was a complicated man, very driven and focused but also deeply religious and a serious donator to charitable causes.

For part of his life he lived at Birley Carr, (Ecclesfield Parish). He bought Page Hall from Mr.Greaves. At the time it was set in very wooded parkland and had a lake and gardens and open views. Details are sparse but he was without a doubt a good example of a Victorian 'self-made' man who took risks, worked hard and succeeded in establishing a firm that was to survive for many generations. It is thought his initial investment in the firm was £100 and at the end of his life he was thought to be worth £100,000.

Sources
1 Sheffield Archives MD 3624 Recollections & Reminisiences of the Dixon family and other familes in connection with them. Charles Dixon 1847.
2 Sheffield Archives, Dixon A142 Mr Dixon's account notebook 1822.
3 Magazine article 'The Goldsmith's Review', James Dixon's and Sons, Silversmiths, Centenary Celebration July 1906 speech by Mr James Willis Dixon.

Silver Eperne presented to James Dixon

TRADE MARK

Knees up - any excuse for a celebration!

Dixon Centenary Luncheon 1906

Centenary celebrations

The celebration that stands out above all others is that which took place in 1906 to celebrate the firm's centenary. It was held at Shire House in Ecclesfield, the home of Mr. James Willis Dixon. On that occasion one of the speakers Mr. Byron Carr (1) described previous celebrations that many present could remember. He said:

'They had had and many of those present had attended several meetings of this kind in the past. Referring to the Rotherham Independent of June 1st 1823 or 83 years ago, he found that the workman of James Dixon-not James Dixon and Sons, then assembled at three o'clock in the morning to celebrate the majority of Mr. William F. Dixon. They formed from the works in Silver Street to the rolling mills in Green Lane, and then went to Birley Edge (The Dixon Family then lived in Birley House) and fired a range of 21 guns. Subsequently they returned to the works, where they arrived safely at nine o'clock in the morning. He supposed they worked. (laughter). They usually did when they had broken a day in that fashion. At five o' clock in the evening a procession was formed, and they went to Birley Edge once more. This was the way the procession was described. The procession was composed of ten cars...They were called Waterloos and they were the only means of communication (transport) between Sheffield and Rotherham. If anyone wanted a Waterloo they went to the Waterloo and they sometimes found the man there and sometimes they did not. If there were only two or three people to go they were kindly told by the man that he would wait until there was a sufficient party... (this could mean the next day). The procession was composed of ten of these Waterloos and there was one gig, one post-chaise and two single horses...Two 18-gallon barrels of beer were disposed of, there was a budding poet present who said that the cautious Cornish place men returned safely to Cornish Place arriving at nine o'clock at night.'

James Willis Dixon's majority

The next event that Mr Carr recalled was of when the present senior partner (James Willis Dixon) attained his majority and he read to the gathering the speech that was made on that occasion by William Fredrick Dixon:

'I perceive it to be an important period in his life, for from this day he need no more sign J. Dixon and Sons per pro, But he was entitled to sign J.Dixon and Sons. I don't conceive that any of you will regret that. I feel that you will be proud to look upon him as one of your future employers. There has always been a good feeling between the employers and employed at Cornish Place which I trust is not likely to be broken. I feel every confidence that our young friend will cultivate that feeling that he will not trample on the rights of those employed and that whilst he strives to do what is right and just to himself and his partners he will pay a due regard to all those who are employed in the

Trams for Dixons outing at Shalesmoor

manufactory. In introducing our young friend as one of your employers, I can say that I have no fear about you being well pleased with him.'

Other Dixon family landmarks

Other past 'knees-up' events referred to in the speeches include the presentation of a portrait to Mr William Fredrick Dixon on May 9th 1870 when he had been a partner for 50 years. In addition there was Mr James Dixon's coming of age at Stumperlowe Hall in 1872. He himself describes this in reminiscences written in 1933 (2).

There was great rejoicing at the Hall and at Cornish Place....The day began with an old canon been fired from the pond bank at Stumperlowe. At 10'o'clock all the workpeople assembled at Ranmoor and headed by the band of the Hallamshire rifles walked in procession to the Hall. All assembled on the lawn in front of the house while the family and a large party of relatives who came to take part in the day...My uncle, Willis Dixon as senior partner in the firm, made a speech and proposed my health and told the workpeople that I was taken into partnership on that day. I replied and then Samuel Wood, the senior clerk presented me with an address. Other speeches followed and I was then suddenly raised by four old women, placed in a chair and carried round. They were the same four women who had chaired my father at Page Hall on his coming of age. I thought once or twice that they would let me drop. The rest of the day was spent in the grounds playing games.

In the evening all the people were entertained to dinner. This was achieved by dividing them into 5 groups so that each group dined at a different hotel. *My father and I visited each hotel in turn and were very tired when it was all over. It had been a very happy day and had fortunately kept fine.*

He later describes how all the Cornish Place workpeople came to see his wedding and how they filled the churchyard.

Mr Henry Isaac Dixon's celebrated 50 years as a partner in similar style to his son's coming of age complete with the band of the Hallamshire rifles and the sports and games in Stumperlowe Park. The work people presented him with an address, a silver tea service and tray, a large clock with Cambridge Chimes and a beautiful carved bracket for the clock to rest on.

In the 1906 celebration speech Mr Byron Carr made mention of the coming of age of both Mr Lennox Dixon and Mr Fawcett 'would be remembered by many of those present and they would recollect the grand time they had had (1889). In 1905 there had been the occasion of Mr Kenneth Dixon's twenty-first birthday when a dinner was held at the Cutlers' Hall at which 900 employees were entertained.

Back to the centenary celebrations

Returning to the 1906 celebration Mr Carr said that Mr Fletcher, the longest serving male employee had asked him to say that 'he felt very proud to be deputed to offer to Mr Dixon, (the same Mr James Willis Dixon) the address and the two silver dishes which expressed their great regard for him and marked the Centenary of the firm and also Mr Dixon's recent marriage. He hoped the relations which had existed between them in the past would with increasing years still continue'. (cheers.) The firm's artist Mr. Tirebuck had in fact illuminated the address and eight men and women from four departments all of whom had between 38 and 59 years service signed it.

By any standards the centenary celebration event was an impressive occasion. It seems the workforce arrived in 22 special tramcars. The event began with a lunch of roast beef and several other meat choices followed by fruit pies and then cheese. Speeches and presentations followed and they went on to participate in various 'athletic sports' such as 220 yards, obstacle race and even a ladies skipping race. I note that one of my great uncles, Harold Cooper took part in the heats. At this time, the firm employed my great grandfather and 3 of his son's. From the list of the employees there were no less than 11 of the Lindley dynasty and 6 of the Baxters. There was a cricket match in the adjoining field of the park. The Cornish Place Choir entertained with a considerable programme as did the 'Cornish Place Centenary Pierrot Troupe.' No further explanation of this is given but I believe a pierrot is a white faced clown. There was also the band of the 1st Hallamshire Rifles and a Punch and Judy act as well as 'an open air minstrel variety entertainment.' Tea included beef and ham and tongue sandwiches as well as cakes and pastries stewed fruit and custard. After tea there was a comic football match and dancing in the large tent, the presentation of the prizes and the singing of the National Anthem. The planned conclusion was at 8.30p.m.

The end of World War 1
The next major event on record is that which was held to greet the end of the First World War which according to the programme was held *in celebration of Victory and Peace on the conclusion of the Great War, 1914-19, given at Stumperlowe Hall on Saturday July 5th 1919 by James Dixon esquire J.P.* (3)

At this event a previous one was recalled when there was a gathering on May 29th 1856 to celebrate the end of the Crimean war. On that occasion a special woodcut was made and printed in the form of a badge on which was recorded the date of the celebration and also above a figure of Peace the motto 'May peace continue and War be known no more'.

At the 1919 event there were 800 employees and their wives present together with several members of the family many of whom, the women included, had returned from war service. Altogether the party was around 1,100-1,200. The luncheon was served in a huge marquee. Later proceedings (4) included sports, entertainments, dancing and comic football as well as music from the 'Comrades of the Great War military band' and singing from the Cornish Place Factory choir. Tribute was paid to the 23 men who had died in the fighting and they were remembered with a minute's silence.

Unfortunately Mrs Dixon was still recovering from influenza and was unable to present the prizes as planned so her daughter Mrs Longden took her place. However the employees obviously did not want Mrs Dixon to be left out so they serenaded her by singing 'Land of Hope and Glory', O God our help in ages past' and the National Anthem. Given there were about 1000 singers it was apparently quite a volume!

Together these events represent a remarkable history of a 'family' firm in that the owners and the employees came together to celebrate events that were of national significance, those that were of significance to the firm and events that were really Dixon or Fawcett events such as the coming of age of the young men who were part of the firm. I think these celebrations were part of what welded the Dixon 'Family' and the employees together, in what was generally mutual respect and loyalty, though this may have been less true after the second world war.

Sources
1. Magazine, The Goldsmith's Review July 1906 pp178-189
2. Sheffield Telegraph Aug 25th and Oct 18th 1933 Reminiscences of Mr. James Dixon.
3. Magazine, The watchmaker, jeweller, silversmith and optician July 1919, *James Dixon and Sons, Sheffield, in war and peace.*
4. Photocopy of the Programme of the event.

A. Fawcett (presumably Alfred) in bowler, Lennox Dixons on the right in cap. Both **Ernest Dixon Fawcett** (son of James Dixon Fawcett) and **Lennox Burton Dixon** (son of James Willis Dixon) celebrated their 21st birthdays together. Charlotte Gregory (centre) was a long serving employee.

TRADE MARK

Labels, Lamps, Liqueur Sets, Lobster Crackers and lots more...

There are occasional jokes at the beginning of the second millennium about retail catalogues like 'Innovations'. People say you wonder how you ever managed without...

When I look at the Dixon's product range as set out in their catalogues covering the period from about 1908 until the 1970's I am astounded not simply at the list of implements available for use in the home but the range on offer.

Those beginning with L demonstrate a random selection in a catalogue (1) that numbers 598 pages of products manufactured by the firm in 1908. *Labels* are made in EPNS and are for bottles of spirits such as whiskey, port, gin etc. *Ladies' card cases and hairbrushes* are produced in silver. You could choose from 9 of the former and 5 of the latter and there are matching combs, cloth brush, hat brush, toilet bottle, puff jar and toilet tray to go with the hairbrushes. Only one *lamp filler*, a spirit can for filling kettle lamps is available obtainable only in EPNS. There are 8 silver table *lamps* and these can also be supplied for less cost in EPNS and all can be adapted for electric light and for any voltage; just one option in EP Britannia metal available for a fraction of the cost of those in silver. The rest of the index for the letter L *includes leather drinking cups, lawn tennis stands and prizes, lemon saws and squeezers, liquid plate polish, liquor frames, loading machines, lobster crackers and scoops, loving cups and lunch frames.* I know the latter as cruets but of course the containers are glass in the frame of silver or EPNS. There are about 120 altogether taking up 8 pages of about A4 size paper and this does not include the pickle frames, oil and vinegar frames, sauce frames or egg frames!

Flatware

Worthy of special mention is the huge range of flatware (knives, forks and spoons) manufactured for sale either individually or in sets of 6 spoons or whatever as well as in canteens. The canteens were beautifully designed either with drawers of removable top trays with a very specific slot for each knife, fork or spoon. In addition to the flatware that was designed simply for an individual to use when eating a meal, there is a huge range of

BEST ELECTRO-PLATED NICKEL SILVER.
(All these patterns are Stamped on both sides.)

No. 4400
KING'S.

No. 4520
QUEEN'S.

No. 4580
VENETIAN.

No. 4810
ITALIAN.

No. 4640
FLORENTINE.

No. 4280
THREADED SHELL.

Feather Edge Range

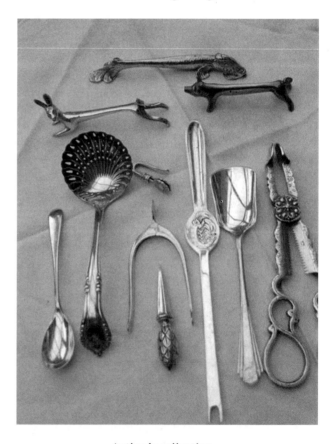

Author's collection

TRADE MARK

44

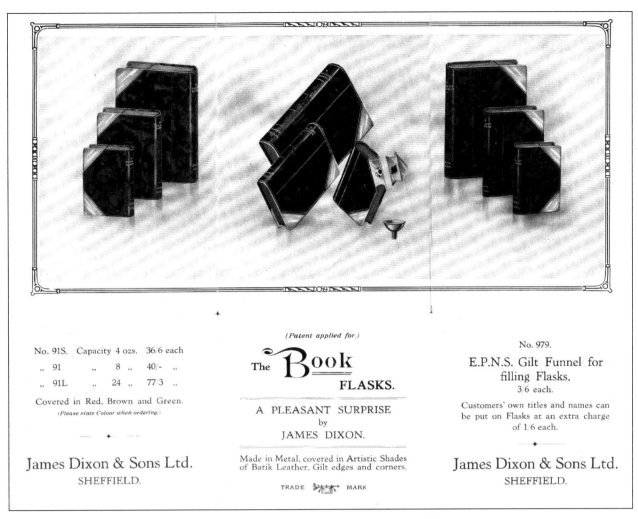

Hips flasks for the American market during prohibition

specialist flatware, some for the table like cake knives, sardine or salad helpers and ginger servers and others for the kitchen such as meat knives. The range of styles is again extensive for tableware cutlery: fiddle, old English, Cromwellian, rat-tail, continental, king's, queen's, Venetian, Italian, Florentine, threaded, Chippendale, Persian, fluted, lily, Louis xiv and Albany.

I have a small personal collection of what is largely EPNS flatware which I have mostly had from the family and which has no particular value. I have however been able to discover by using one of these product catalogues that I am the proud owner of a salt spoon, lobster scoop, ice tongues complete with cutter for ice or sugar, mustard spoon, bread fork, pickle fork and jam spoon plus a few items whose use I had already guessed at. I also have three knife rests in the shape of a hare, a pig and a fish.

Some products were made for specific customers and marked accordingly. I have a set of teaspoons that have come down through the family which were made for the Savoy Hotel in London. Each has on it the Savoy coat of arms and they are beautifully boxed.

Self Pouring Teapot

One very popular line was a self-pouring teapot which was originally designed by J.J. Royles of Manchester and patented in 1886. They were still making it up to the World War 2 and Milo Dixon suggested in 1962 that they would still make it but were unable to find anyone who could make the tight fitting cylinder essential to make it work. As far as I can imagine it, it seemed to work a little on the same scientific principle as a modern automatic tea-maker alarm which some of us have on our bedside tables. The tea was dropped into the pot and a long cylinder attached to the lid was placed inside until the tea had brewed. It was then lifted and with a finger placed over the hole at the top slowly pushed down to force a cup of tea out through the short spout. (2)

TRADE MARK

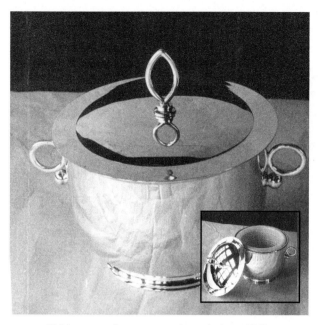

Tableware of a more modern design, 1962

SYP teapot

Simple yet perfect was yet another model made in electro-plated Britannia metal up until about 1930. Balanced on its back with spout in the air the tea was brewed in a special compartment divided off by a filter from the main body of the pot. After the recommended 6 minutes for brewing the pot could be turned upright and the leafless tea poured normally. Who needed tea bags?

Pocket Flasks for the USA

One range of goods is particularly interesting from a social history perspective. When I first borrowed one of these product catalogues (3) from Barrie he pointed out to me the page that illustrated the pocket flask section.

Some of the illustrations are genuine pocket flasks; they might actually fit into someone's pocket. However there are also some larger containers one of which would hold a capacity of 1 gallon (USA) or just over 6 pints in imperial

measurements. It looks like what I remember as a petrol can that many motorists had in the car even in the 1950's before there was a filling station on every corner. Next to it is another can with a capacity of a pint. This can is divided into two sections and labelled 'water' one side and 'milk' the other. Barrie said it was common knowledge that these cans were produced for the American market and were for the purpose of carrying something a little stronger than either of the labels suggested. It is possible that these products were introduced by Dixon's in the 1920's specifically because of prohibition. I understand that 'a blind eye' was often turned by the authorities to enforcing the law if alcohol consumption was in private.

In an earlier catalogue covering the period up to the First World War is an even more surprising additional loose leaflet advertising a product range that I feel certain must have been for this purpose. They were called 'book flasks'. These came in 3 sizes and 3 colours of red, brown and green that looked like books with bindings of batik leather with gilt edges and corners. It was possible to remove one of the corners and there was the nozzle through which the liquid could be poured. It was also possible to buy a gilt funnel. The title on the books was 'A Pleasant Surprise' by James Dixon. Customers own titles and names could be put on the flasks at an extra charge of 1/6 each. The smallest one would lodge in a pocket and the larger ones could easily be hidden amongst other books in your car or office. A fellow researcher tells me that he has seen a similar 'book' advertised that was given the title 'A Swallow's Return'!

At a later date the firm produced some authentic working replicas of muzzle loading powder flasks as made for the Americas over a century previously. These were made in antiqued satin finish on copper with polished brass spring loaded powder measure. One is illustrated with a canon and flag, another with a hunting scene and a third with fluted leaf. (See chapter on guns)

Sources

1   Private collection Dixon's catalogue 1908-11
2   Sheffield telegraph Saturday September 15th 1973
3   Catalogue belonging to the author

Marks, Assay and Trade

Assaying

Precious metals have the longest tradition of consumer protection in British history, about 700 years. The hallmark as it is called must consist of a sponsor's mark, the fineness number and the mark of the Assay office which has tested it and which guarantees that it conforms to a specified legal standard of purity. Until 1999 a date letter was also required but this is no longer compulsory though most offices including Sheffield stamp it on unless asked not to do so. To assay is to analyse the components in the article to ensure that the article reaches the approved standard. For sterling silver the minimum is 92.5%. There are assay offices in London, Sheffield, Birmingham and Edinburgh.

A firm like Dixon's would be registered with a particular assay office. In their case this was Sheffield. Their specific sponsor mark would then appear on the article along with the number that indicates the minimum precious metal content. The shape of the shield indicates whether it is silver, gold or platinum. Silver is always printed on an oval shield. The assay office mark would also appear. Until 1975 this for Sheffield would be a crown and thereafter the rose.

Despite challenges over the years to do away with assay marking, including one from the European Community in 2003, it is a process that has both maintained and consistently protected standards and prevented fraud.

Both Lennox Dixon and Milo Dixon are amongst those who have served as guardians of the Sheffield assay office.

Trade Marks

In the 1906 Centenary booklet it is stated that the trademarks of the firm are a 'trumpet with banner' and the same in combination with the word 'Dixon'. It seems that from 1828-33 things were simply marked 'Dixon & Son'. The first corporate mark of the trumpet and banner was granted in 1879, and the second with the name added in 1890. (1) However in another pamphlet (2) it is claimed that the trumpet with banner trademark was officially registered in 1881 though had been in use prior to that. It doesn't appear in the 1876 Sporting Catalogue.

In the works manager's notebook (3) it states that in 1921 Mr Lennox instructed 'GB' to get some new marks. These were the James Dixon and Sons written in a semi circle with Sheffield underneath and EPBM underneath that. The other was a slightly different version of the trumpet mark. Several products were marked but it is recorded in the same source that some customers complained and the new marks were discontinued. An example I guess of resistance to change. This appears to be coming from

TRADE MARK

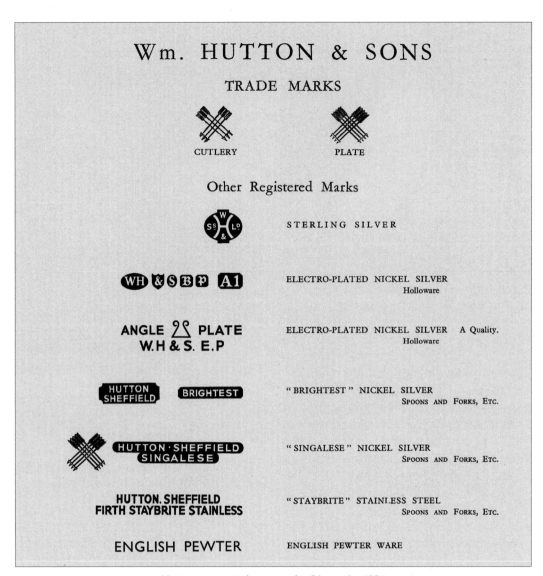

Wm. HUTTON & SONS

TRADE MARKS

CUTLERY   PLATE

Other Registered Marks

STERLING SILVER

ELECTRO-PLATED NICKEL SILVER
Holloware

ANGLE PLATE
W.H & S. E.P

ELECTRO-PLATED NICKEL SILVER   A Quality.
Holloware

HUTTON SHEFFIELD   BRIGHTEST

"BRIGHTEST" NICKEL SILVER
SPOONS AND FORKS, ETC.

HUTTON·SHEFFIELD
SINGALESE

"SINGALESE" NICKEL SILVER
SPOONS AND FORKS, ETC.

HUTTON. SHEFFIELD
FIRTH STAYBRITE STAINLESS

"STAYBRITE" STAINLESS STEEL
SPOONS AND FORKS, ETC.

ENGLISH PEWTER

ENGLISH PEWTER WARE

Huttons were taken over by Dixons in 1931

outside the firm, however it could be that such customer feedback supported feelings within.

In May 1923 Mr Fawcett ordered that all goods made in Britannia metal must have the new marks on them and all the old marks were to be collected in. All plated goods for the colonies were to have the new marks where possible but 'country orders to be marked as before as there is an objection to Dixon in full by the customers.'

In Lennox 's papers (4) there is reference in May 1924 to a firm trying to 'steal' Dixon's trade by calling themselves J&J.E. Dixon and advertising Dixon's plate. No further details are given other than that the real Dixon's were disputing it.

Trade description issues

Up until the 1920's the trademark in essence was to tell people who had made the product. Also stamped on it would be the assay mark or EPNS.

In Lennox' papers there is some correspondence with the public analysis office in Surrey Street, Sheffield. As I understand it certain products

had been sent to this office and also to a firm in Birmingham for testing in relation to tarnishing and corrosion particularly from salt and vinegar. In November 1929 a John Evans wrote to Lennox that various tests had been done and that all the products except for 'staybrite' steel had been affected. He added that tarnish was due to the formation of a film of sulphide silver on the surface that is a chemical action. The conclusion was that only 'staybrite' could be marked 'stainless' and that other products could be marked 'stain resisting'.

How further decisions were made I have not as yet been able to discover but at the beginning of the catalogue in use in the 1970's there are various trademarks that seem to me to be a consequence of these 1920's 'tests' and that marks were adopted for different types of metal used. (See advert on opposite page)

One trademark has 4 parts to it: an NS rotated 90

TRADE MARK

JAMES DIXON & SONS, Ltd.

TRADE MARKS

Other Registered Marks

STERLING SILVER	JD&S
ELECTRO-PLATED NICKEL SILVER Holloware	EP JD&S
"CORNISH" NICKEL SILVER SPOONS AND FORKS, ETC.	NS DIXON
"RESISTARN" NICKEL SILVER SPOONS AND FORKS, ETC.	NS DIXON RESISTARN
"STAYBRITE" STAINLESS STEEL SPOONS AND FORKS, ETC.	DIXON FIRTH STAYBRITE STAINLESS
"NO-RUS" CUTLERY	"NO-RUS" FIRTH STAINLESS
"CORNISH" PEWTER WARE	Cornish Pewter

degrees in a small oval followed by Dixon followed by the trumpet followed by the word 'resistarn'. So here was a product that could not be described as stainless but could be described as resisting tarnishing. Stainless steel spoons and forks carried the 'staybrite' name and even had the name 'Firth' on it. Firth Brown's was the firm where 'staybrite' steel was invented just before the First World War and it was the first rust proof stainless steel to be made. The kitchens of HMS Sheffield were made from it and there is a pub at Lodge Moor in Sheffield still there to-day which is called 'The Shiney Sheff' inspired I believe by the metal and the ship. However in 1975 Milo records that he told George Patterson not to mark anymore spoons and forks 'Firth Staybrite' only 'Dixon stainless'

There was also a ' "No-Rus" Firth Stainless' mark and finally marks for different metals. JD&S was the mark for sterling silver and Cornish Pewter for pewter ware. Electro-plated nickel silver hollow-ware was EP rotated ninety degrees followed by JD&S and the trumpet. Spoons and forks were marked NS rotated ninety degrees followed by DIXON and the trumpet. All these trademarks are illustrated and are taken from contemporary catalogues.

However the trademark that is most recognised and identifies today a Dixon's product is without question the trumpet and banner.

Sources
1. Centenary souvenir James Dixon & Sons, Sheffield 1906 p.33
2. The Journal of the Arms and Armour Society Vol. V, No 3 Sept 1965
3. Sheffield Archives Dixon's A192 Notebook containing extracts from documents, notes, memoranda etc 1896-1923
4. Sheffield Archives Dixon's A186 Correspondence of Lennox Dixon.

TRADE MARK

Night Watchman and Other Ancillary Employees

There were many jobs within the works that were not directly related to the manufacturing output. In to-day's world many of these jobs would be outsourced including that of the night watchman. He would now be an employee of a security firm. In all probability the maintenance of buildings would also be outsourced whereas in the nineteenth and early twentieth century Dixon's like many firms employed even their own joiners and bricklayers. On the wages list in 1916 there also appears a lift attendant, kitchen workers and sitting room workers. This last group were two women whose wages were half that of the bricklayers. I assume they looked after the 'staff' dining room.

White-collar managerial employees were referred to as 'staff' as opposed to the workpeople. In the centenary booklet (1) there is a photograph of between 30 and 40 men. The photograph is simply captioned 'Staff at Sheffield'. All are wearing suits and many have quite stiff collars and all are wearing ties. This is 1906.

Another photograph showing both the works and the workpeople pictures several hundred men and women, many wearing 'aprons'. The photograph is captioned 'View of works and workpeople' (2). You can stand to-day where the photographer stood and see much the same scene, sadly though only the buildings without any of the work people. The photograph taken in 2004 does however show some of the present residents and users of the building. (See overpage) The night watchman would have been quite an important role as the works would always have contained valuable raw materials such as silver and gold as well having a large showroom of finished products and great quantities of part finished items.

In an early record book (3) there is an account of the recruiting of a retiring police constable William Baxter as the night watchman. References were obtained from the Chief Constable. The job involved working 12-hour shifts 7 days a week alternate weeks and on the alternate week Monday 7.30p.m. to 6a.m. and on the Sunday 10p.m. to 6a.m.

By the 1960's there had been little change as the night watchman then worked 6 nights a week Sunday to Friday doing 12 hour shifts. On Saturday nights the caretaker did one week and Dick Axelby who was a silver chaser did the alternate week. Graham Axelby, Dicks's son told me that his father found the experience quite 'spooky'. As they walked round the building which they were supposed to do 3 or 4 times a

Dick Axelby, night watchman once a forthnight

night they would hear all kinds of creaks and strange noises. (4) This change to the caretaking arrangement may have been as a result of John Bower leaving. He had been night watchman for 29 years though had worked for the firm for 46 years. Fred Lees was appointed on November 8th and resigned on November 11th. George Ellis was then given the post and he started on November 14th earning £4/15/- a week for his 72 hours.

In May 1896 a gas maker was taken on. He was given a job description which included such

Workers, 1906, below residents 2004

TRADE MARK

clauses as,

1. To stack the coal required for gas making so as to leave room to walk where required.
2. To charge the retorts as often as required to supply the factory with gas.
3. All the valves must be clean and in proper working order and the siphons regularly pumped.

There were 11 clauses all together and the conditions of employment included a weekly wage of 30/- and a short holiday in the summer by arrangement. There was also a condition that if the factory were ever without gas a fine of 1/- would be imposed. It was apparently possible if there were any problems, to turn off the internal supply and switch to the gas company source. A Mr Coulson agreed to these terms in May 1896.

The Timekeeper was a very important role so much so that he had a house actually on the site. The house still stands to-day though is now modern apartments. The timekeeper's office was right beside the main gate and can be seen left of the archway in the chapter on 'Visitors'. In 1952 when Barrie began his apprenticeship the timekeeper was a Herbert Ratherham. He was apparently a rather gloomy character, so much so that if you wished him 'Good morning' he would rap back at you *What's good about it?'* He was though a regular member of the Fishing Club. The clocking in system involved numbered discs with a hole in them. Each number represented a worker. As you arrived you took your disc and dropped it into a special box. Exactly at starting time Herbert removed the box and after that you were late and wages were adjusted accordingly. It was quite a powerful role and as can be seen in the section on warehouse girls, the timekeeper carried a lot of responsibility. In 1937 Mr Constantine recorded that, 'the time book shows that those to whom it was necessary to speak concerning the many times they arrived late in the mornings have mended their ways'.

The Caretaker was a kind of back up role for relieving the watchman and the timekeeper and seemed to be recruited from within the existing workforce. In 1937 Arthur Spye who was a hollow-ware buffer as well as the caretaker left Dixon's and was replaced by G. Gabbitas who was also a hollow-ware buffer. His first task was to report on the condition and position of the fire extinguishers. George Gabbitas did the job for 23 years giving up the job because the house

was unsuitable now that his children were growing up.

GB Ibbotson who worked in the flask department replaced him in June 1959. He was a young man, married with a three year old child. Minor repairs were agreed to for the house and the writer was pleased that a young couple could move from rented rooms into their own home. On December 23rd. some silver goods were found in the canteen cellar and these were left and checked daily just after Christmas. Most workers were off work until after the new year so when it was found on Dec 31st that some of these goods had disappeared the CID were called in and searched the building. Missing goods were found in the caretaker's cellar and he was charged with theft. (4)

There is record in Mr Constantine's notes of an accident in May 1921. It appears there was a team of people responsible for whitewashing the workshops. When working in the casting shop of the Britannia Metal Dept. Mrs Tadwell received burns to her face and injuries to her eyes and mouth. She had several operations and on her return to work, found a job in the 'boil' shop, the boil being an acid vat. Finding her a job was presumably an act of generosity though in to-day's compensation culture it sounds like out of the frying pan and into the fire!

I believe there were many other ancillary roles about which there are no detailed records or stories that I have heard so far other than carpenters, bricklayers and handyman appearing on wages lists. Barrie thinks that in his time a joiner with a workshop on the premises was partly self employed, partly doing work for Dixon's

Sources
1. Centenary souvenir James Dixon & Sons, Sheffield 1906 p.17
2. Op Cit p.32
3. Sheffield Archives Dixon's A192 notebook containing extracts from documents, notes on memoranda, abstracts from agreements, extracts covering 1896-1923
4. Sheffield Archives Dixon's A195 volume marked 'cash' book but containing memoranda and notes 1952-62

Timekeeper's Cottage Today

Overseas - on Every Continent?

By 1850 no country could compare with Britain in terms of the volume of cheap manufactured goods produced. At this time 25% of the world's trade was going through British ports. (1) Britain was particularly successful in South America and in India. 1851 was the date of the Great Exhibition in London and the relatively new railway companies ran cheap excursion trains enabling people to see more of what was possible.

In 1869, the Suez Canal was opened and this shortened the distance from England to India by six weeks and thousands of miles. Trade was the driving force behind the Empire and centred on India. Exports included cotton, woollen and metal goods. From India some of these were exported to China and tea from China came to England. Presumably as far as Dixon's was concerned tea from China or India stimulated the demand for teapots and tea services in the home country. Africa was also being opened up in the mid 1800's. In the 1860's diamonds were discovered there and in the 1880's, gold.

James Willis Dixon, grandson of the founder was born in New York in 1838. This suggests that at this stage in the firm's development there was already a presence in the United States and in a letter (2) to a Mrs Joan Springer written in 1971 Milo Dixon says that his grandfather was born in the States when his father was travelling for the firm. Therefore they were in the States in the 1830's. There is a book of handwritten copies of letters (3) from Willis Fredrick Dixon to his brother in America, the earliest of which seem to be at the beginning of the expansion of the firm's exports to America. They are, I believe from William Fawcett Dixon to James Willis Dixon who were brothers in law. The writing is not always easy to decipher and they are a mixture of work issues and personal news. The first is written in 1835 and is about orders for casks and flasks. It seems that a company in the States has asked for some kind of special deal. This prompts the response *your father thinks it would never do to give any house an advantage over their neighbours. We had better allow one or two houses to close with us for (?illegible). The glory of conducting our business has always been in the straight forward and upright course'.*

The letters confirm receipt of orders such as 'Cupson's and Coupland of Philadelphia' order for £60 (1836) and later the same year remittance from S. Davies of Baltimore.

The personal news includes 'Mrs Fawcett presented me with another daughter last Monday and mother and child are doing very well.' In another the writer comments that 'your father returned from Harrogate but is not very well and I am very busy, excuse me not saying more this month.'

One batch of letters written around 1879 concerns the attempted purchase of a piece of land in Texas. These are fairly typical solicitors' letters where the whole transaction seems to have got stuck due to the death of the vendor and a wrangle with the authorities in Texas because taxes had not been paid. There is no indication of whether this was ever brought to completion.

Other archive material mentions that they were trading with the East India Company in the 1840's, shipping cutlery and receiving products like tin and copper. (5) Specific mention is made of Hong Kong and Manila in 1846. South America also gets a mention, Rio de Janeiro in 1841 and also Valpariso.

Australia and New Zealand
It is also certain that there was a presence in Australia by the beginning of the twentieth century. Showrooms existed in both Sydney and Melbourne by 1908. There is a remarkable record in the archives which contains the original letters written by Allan Hedderly, Dixon's representative covering Australia and New Zealand. The record (6) is the account of his first attempts to establish a base in Adelaide and is remarkable for the frequency with which he wrote and the detail that he included. His writing is very legible and I have quoted substantial sections as I think it gives clear insights to the challenges faced by these pioneer 'salesmen.' He was actually away from home 9 months.

TRADE MARK

Representatives, 1906 Mr Allan Hedderly (top) in 1898 went on a nine month trip to Austrialia and New Zealand

On March 29th he is already on board the RMSS 'Orient' sailing via Naples and the Suez Canal (April) with bad weather expected in the 'Bay'. He writes that he expects to arrive Diego Garcia in a few hours and that he will post the letter via his wife because he is unable to purchase stamps at this remote island and probably the postal services will charge double 'although sometimes they deliver free'. He writes on May 16th from the York Hotel in Adelaide having arrived on May12th:

'Started on business the next morning and cleared my samples through customs, engaged offices and unpacked all the goods and have half of them laid out on my tables ready for inspection and hope by tomorrow to have every piece unpapered. I have 2 rooms on a second floor, could not get anything lower down that would suit and consequently I am rather stiff today with carrying the goods upstairs. I am however very fortunate in getting assistance from a Mr Lynn, late with ? Collins being out of employment. I have arranged for him to assist

me as he is well acquainted with our goods and knows his work. I am a good deal more forward than I should have been otherwise, in fact I shall have to do same everywhere as it would take over a week for one to unpack and lay out the patterns. I pay 35/- a week for offices and have tables placed all around the rooms and down the centre and it takes about 120 feet long and 3 feet wide to show all the patterns at all decently... The duty and carriage of goods to offices is £118/16/0 and I get full amount back for samples not left here. The duties are different from last journey and several alterations rather beneficial to me as I can get the rebate 3 days after the goods are placed on board or in bond whereas last time the customs at Melbourne had to sign a paper showing the goods were in that colony before the rebate was forwarded and that of necessity caused great delay. Everyone here complains of the dullness of trade. It has never been so bad before. In fact Adelaide seems to be in a state of bankruptcy and many people have lost their all in the Commercial bank and a great want of confidence in every branch is experienced... I shall not make any appointments till the arrival of the rest of the patterns, invoices of which I got on my arrival here. The advice notes I regret to find have not been sent. I presume they will come by the P&O with the books. I should have preferred them here now as I shall have Wednesday and Thursday for writing and shall now use ordinary paper. I am writing this on a Sunday as the mail goes out tomorrow... I am sticking hard and trust although trade is bad to be able to send some orders soon as I feel confident that my samples will compel customers to buy. Directly I finish here I shall take first steamer to Melbourne and push up to Townsville in Queensland if possible as their trade is good and I shall stand a chance of getting orders.'

He had to take another room because he needed more space and started to obtain a variety of orders though some people thought the Britannia metal goods were too expensive. He went on to say:

'We must send more catalogues to houses

direct'. Apparently rival firms get in if the 'houses' have not heard from Dixon's for sometime. He passes on all the comments from visiting buyers whether they place orders with him or not. He goes on to say: *'All the above names should be placed in a book for future Australian guidance and we must pay these people attention in sending photos and new illustrations direct particularly ironmongers and jewellers as they take care of these illustrations and also like us to post them up with the information and where it goes through the London Houses. They get sent to Melbourne for distribution and never reach the proper quarter.'*

He goes on to say that all articles that are sent here which are receptacles for food such as jam or sugar pots must have lids because of the flies. He writes of a proposed exhibition next year at which he thinks they should exhibit and suggests a particular piece which he says, was in Conolly's window which is of huntsman on horseback and hounds. He seems to think there is a possibility of the commission for the Melbourne Cup. He goes on to tell of the possibility of the opening up of the rail to New South Wales. He goes on to write *'I believe that the time is not far hence when the colonies will keep one man well employed but shall be able to form a sounder judgement when I return'*

His next letter is from the Scotts Hotel in Melbourne where he had the Harris Scarfe buyer Mr Williams for 6 hours. It is now July and he writes that he is of the opinion 'that the journey should be taken every other year or thereabouts and this would be cheaper than having an agency out here and also not offend customers as they are rather nasty at houses of our sort having stock here but do not so much object to the travelling (representative) and having no stated office or residence.' He continues by suggesting that when next this journey is done that 3 months at least should be given to Melbourne, 'the tastes of Melbourne being more advanced than Adelaide, cheap oval patterns in Britannia Metal seems the most saleable. He then moved on to Sydney and Brisbane and then to New Zealand where he finds that there is a 5% duty on all goods and that trade is very bad indeed. In August he writes that he sincerely hopes to be home by Christmas and in fact docks back in England on December 23rd having done a nine-month sales trip. He complains that telegrams did not reach him and that he will

come as soon as possible and bring with him details of all accounts.

In the 1920's there is considerable correspondence in Lennox Dixon's papers (7) concerning the possibility of setting up an Australian Company. The proposal seems to have been made by a J.K. Merriott and as far as I can make out from the letters that Lennox wrote, the proposal seemed a bit along the lines of a modern franchise agreement. Merriott suggested the company be called James Dixon and Son's (Australia) Propriety Ltd. Half the company was to be owned by the Merriott interest and the other half by Dixon's. I am uncertain whether this went ahead but there were concerns that sooner or later local interests would squeeze British manufactures out of Australia and tariffs on imported goods had already been threatened. Certainly Dixon's still had interests in Australia in the 1950's because the embargo placed on imported goods is partly why Barrie extended his skills from originally training as a flatware finisher to working with his father on hollow-ware. Work on flatware was scarce in the 1950's because of Australia's embargo on imported goods.

In 1968 Milo Dixon records that Peter Deardon flew to Australia 'to consult Geoff' and back via the USA and that he was away for 3 weeks.

Europe, Uncle and Nephew
There are a series of letters in the archives (8) which concern a journey made in 1858. I believe this is a business trip undertaken by William Fawcett of the second generation together with James Willis Dixon his nephew and therefore of the third generation. Willis wrote from Amsterdam in April that the crossing was so stormy that 'the captain dare not take the ship over the bar of the river and consequently was obliged to take us round Dordrecht 60 miles out of the regular way. The tide had been higher around Rotterdam than it had been for very many years'. At the Bath Hotel what 'struck our attention was a cream jug (1314 or 1413) which must have been in use 20 to 25 years'. I assume from this that it was a cream jug made by the firm and that the numbers were the pattern numbers. He has to conclude in haste as 'Uncle' is waiting for him to go for a walk. They seem in Amsterdam to have acquired orders for jugs, sugar bowls and table spoons.

In The Hague they set up a contract with a firm

TRADE MARK

55

called D. Boer and Sons on Royal Bazaar and received orders for kettles, cruets, cream jugs and soap boxes. The order list concludes with the note that: 'I think this house will become a good one for us in plated as well as other goods...Mr Boer will be coming to England in a month or two and may probably come to Sheffield...Most of the people speak a little English or French or German so we get along very well'

From there they went to Germany, William Fawcett writes 'arrived yesterday and on our way to Hamburg found the place so much improved by the railway and other things that we resolved to remain half a day.' He alludes to Willis being anxious about some dishes as he had promised them this month. A few days later they were in Berlin. All the orders include comments on the kind of shop, impressions of the owner with regard to their reliability. The shops ranged from lamp dealer to gun shops and saddlers. They decided at the end of April that it 'will not be desirable' to go to Vienna. They also went to 'Leipsic' and Stuttgard.

In Hanover they received an order from Franz Beckmann whom they described as a first class lamp dealer. In May he wrote saying 'The proposals of war cause me to annul for the present the order for patterns which I gave you on April 23rd when you were here, for under these circumstances, I have no chance of success in these articles, which are new to me. I shall take the liberty after some time of addressing you again and sending you an order'.

James Dixon, brother to James Willis Dixon

In his reminiscences (9) he describes travelling for the firm in Germany before the construction of the railways. He tells of the journey between Bremen and Hamburg which was made by diligence. (a horse drawn vehicle).

It took all night and was like going back to the Middle Ages. The driver had a wonderful cocked hat and feather and of course a horn. Four persons sat inside the coupe and we got as much sleep as we could sitting up. Each of these towns had its own coinage. We left Bremen about 8pm and sometime in the night were roused up in Prussia for examination of luggage and for drinks of coffee or beer. Here we found Prussian money, the old thaler, value 3/-. We crossed the Elbe on a ferry between Harburg and Hamburg arriving in the latter place in the early morning.

Here again we had a different coinage the Hamburg shilling. It was not until sometime after the Franco-Prussian war that Bismark made a new coinage for all Germany.

French Connections

The first journey to Paris on behalf of the firm was undertaken by William Fawcett, son in law of the founder and the latter's youngest son Henry Isaac Dixon. This journey was made by steamer from London Bridge to Boulogne and then by diligence to Paris. There were practically no footpaths in Paris and oil lamps swung across the streets. Henry Isaac went there regularly after the Treaty of Commerce made with Louis Napolean. It seems he became highly trusted by his customers and in 1870 one of them hastily departed from Paris as the Prussian army was marching on it. He made for Sheffield and at Cornish Place entrusted all his cash to Mr. Dixon until the war was over. (10)

In contrast in 1864 the firm was facing threats of legal action from a firm in France called 'Christoffle'.(11) As far as I can work out these are solicitor's letters and the French manufacturer is accusing them of having copied a pattern for a double salt cellar. Dixon's response states that 'we have designers and modellers for our manufactures one of them has bought to us the double salt cellar frames of No 443 and we have adopted it not knowing that it has been copied from any pattern existing and if we were pirating Mr Christofles patterns knowingly, now would we be fool enough to send them to France where they are exclusively known to Mr Christofle's customers'. The solicitor seems to suggest that all they have to do is prove the pattern existed prior to Mr. Christofle's and comments that the latter is jealous of Dixon's metal and has always been. When and how this was resolved I have not yet discovered.

The Carribean

The photograph shows Milo Dixon on the extreme right about to board the free inaugral flight in VC10, the new service in 1968 from London to Bermuda, Antigua, Barbados, Trinidad and Guiyana. In his works diary and dated May 13th-23rd 1968 he writes of this flight, 'called on about 20 shops. Only about 2 in each place likely to be any good'. He describes the plane as a wonderful aircraft.(12)

TRADE MARK

Inaugural BOAC VC10 service, London-Bermuda-Antigua-Barbados-Trinadad-Guyana 1968. Milo Dixon far left

The changes in transport

In the 1906 Centenary brochure there are individual portraits of 13 men who are described as 'Representatives'. One of these is Allan Hedderley whose Australian trip is described above though the only one mentioned in the text is Thomas Heeley because he succeeded his grandfather and father as the representative in the North of England and Scotland. His grandfather was in post for 50 years, his father for 40 years and in 1906 Thomas had achieved 30 years. Some of these representatives would have worked in England, Scotland and Ireland like Thomas Heeley and others like Alan Heddley would have travelled to distant places.

It is also worthy of note that in every generation it seems that one of the Dixon or Fawcett family also travelled extensively to promote the firms products. Henry Isaac started at the age of 6. It is recorded in his obituary that he accompanied his father, the founder on one of his searches for orders. The year was 1826 and the carriage was well stocked with 'order-enticing' samples and pulled by four post horses to Barnsley. They then went to York and in easy stages to Scarborough and the North East Coast. He later as a boy went with his father to Southport and Manchester using the same means of travel.

He himself later used the train to go south from Derby to Birmingham and the rest of the journey to Plymouth and the West Country, was done by coach.

Ireland

He later travelled to Ireland. Starting from Liverpool he first worked the city of Belfast and then a number of other towns. Travelling by coach he saw a great deal of the country. During the great famine he collected in Sheffield, a considerable sum of money that he sent for the relief of the starving populations of Skibberean and other places.

Coach to Air-travel

It does seem that within the first hundred years of their existence Dixon's managed to establish a presence in every continent. The original James Dixon must have taken days to get to London to promote the firm's wares. Journeys by sea to remote parts of the world took months and by 1968, they were flying between continents. One little note in Milo's diary for 1962 reports that A. Snowden had showed him a pair of Muzzle Loading pistols which had been found after many years in the top 'flask' shop. It was thought that they were carried by members of the firm when travelling by road'.

TRADE MARK

Sources

1 Fraser Rebecca, A people's history of Britain, London Chatto and Windus 2003 p. 536
2 Sheffield Archives Dixon's A447 Papers of Milo Dixon c.1862-75 incl. memoranda book 1962-7
3 Sheffield archives Dixon's B40 Copy letter book, comprising letters from J. Dixon to the USA incl. letters to his brother Sept 1835-May 1841
4 Sheffield Archives Dixon's A251 Bundle of correspondence from Texas 1875-1 9 0 7 Sheffield Archives Dixon's A251 Bundle of correspondence from Texas 1875-1907
5 Sheffield Archives Dixon's A73 Minute Book 1844
6 Sheffield Archives Dixon's A90 Copy letter book. Copies of letters from Australia and New Zealand sent by Dixon's Agent 1896
7 Sheffield Archives Dixon's A186 Correspondence of Lennox Dixon
8 Sheffield Archives Dixon's B298 Continental Journey Sheets and letters April 1859.
9 Sheffield Telegraph Oct. 7th 1933, Reminiscences of Mr. James Dixon a former Master Cutler
10 Sheffield Telegraph November 25 1912 Obituary Mr H.I. Dixon
11 Sheffield Archives Dixon's A298 Bundle of correspondence from Christoffle and Co to Dixon's 1864.
12 Sheffield Archives Dixon's B447 Papers of Milo Dixon c.1962-75 incl. memoranda book 1962-73

No. 762
Double Salts.
Blue Glass Linings.
12/- per pair.

The double salt cellar of the type in the dispute with Mr Christofle, 1864

On the Admiralty, War Office, India Office Lists, etc.

TELEGRAMS:
"Dixon, Sheffield"
"James Dixon, Lud, London"
"Amdix, Melbourne"
"Hutton, Sheffield"
"Silversmiths (Lud), London"
———
Codes used: A.B.C. Bentley's

TRADE MARKS

TELEPHONES:
SHEFFIELD - - - - 21221
LONDON - Central 5113, 5114
MELBOURNE - Central 907
SYDNEY - - - - MA 4763

SHOW ROOMS

SHEFFIELD : Cornish Place

MELBOURNE : Box 182B G.P.O., Carson Place, 285A, Little Collins Street

LONDON : Cornish House, 14, St. Andrew Street, Holborn Circus, E.C. 4.

SYDNEY : Box 792G G.P.O., 430/1, The Grace Buildings, York, King & Clarence Streets

LAUSANNE   CAPE TOWN   JOHANNESBURG   DURBAN

TRADE MARK

Pay - The Weekly Ritual

At Dixon's in the 1950's getting the weekly pay was something of a ritual. As I understand it the workforce lined up. Names were called in turn, alphabetically by department. Each person was handed a small round box which was rather like an egg cup with a lid split in half. Inside the box would be the wages in cash. The notes were carefully folded in half and the coins were in the bottom and could be tipped out through the half lid. In addition there was a written record of the payment in the form of a pay slip. The box was returned to a little window, an action which presumably indicated that you had received the correct amount. I assume this was how it had been done from time in memoriam. Mr Tetley who worked at Dixon's after World War II remembers the Christmas bonuses (a week's wages) were handed out by Milo Dixon.

Piecework, Datal or Salaried

There were three basic systems through which people earned their pay. Some of the employees were paid under the datal system which meant that there was a basic fixed rate for a day's work. Others were on piecework which meant that they were paid according to the amount of work that they did.

However even the pieceworkers had a small weekly rate as employees of Dixon's and whatever they earned as piece workers was on top of this. The unions negotiated the rates of pay for both datal and pieceworkers. In addition it was possible for particularly difficult jobs for a worker to negotiate a slightly higher rate with the works' manager. In Harry's time and in Barrie's early years this was Mr. Constantine who had worked his way up from the shop floor to become works' manager and a director. I understand that such attempts were like getting blood out of a stone and that he was a formidable man who rarely gave them their extra few pence an item. In addition to this there was a set rate for bonuses. So if for instance they had finished six dozen table spoons at a 1/- a dozen they might then get a bonus of 5% of 6/-.

At the end of each process the work was checked and signed over. Each worker was given a copy from like a duplicate invoice book that recorded the work (s)he was handing over, the amount paid and the job number. Obviously the firm's copy remained in the book. Barrie's department always handed work over on a Wednesday and were then paid on Friday. This may have been a Wednesday job for all departments.

There are obviously issues around the two systems of datal and piecework. Some skills obviously didn't lend themselves to piece work and were therefore datal jobs. Piecework tended to be for the skills of trades like buffers, burnishers or finishers all of whom could receive a fixed sum for each article completed. Having said that, Dick Axelby's was in his early days as a silver chaser, on piecework. There were periods in the year when he would have to 'sign on' because work was so short and this was often true during the autumn. A chaser only worked on sterling silver or Britannia metal and the fancy goods shops would purchase all their Christmas stock in the late summer and would not reorder until after Christmas. It would seem that in some years he was only fully employed from about Easter to September. It was a good week to take home £3. There were obviously advantages to being in a skill area that dealt with EPNS products as well as sterling silver.

There was also the group known as 'staff' who were what became known as 'white collar' workers. Certainly the chief designer would have been in this group as well as some with management roles. In 1937 there were 35 men and 11 women who were classed as staff. Mr Constantine reports that their salaries or wages in 1937 were increased. The salaried received £10 a year more and the men paid weekly 4/- a week and the woman 2/- a week. In the picture on the opposite page, the man 3rd on the left, spectacles and umbrella was known throughout the firm as 'Barnes 1'. This nickname (his real name was Dick Barnes) was aquired as a result of always being the first on the list in this pay ritual. The pay clerk began it by calling Barns 1". I understand the datal workers were always in there in good time and the piece workers would rush in at the last moment! In 1919 both Mr Constantine and Mr. Deardon the two non family directors received identical salaries of £41/13/4d per month. This was about double

Dixon's cellars been used as air raid shelters, WWII. Note difference in dress between 'staff' and 'workers' The very tall man on the left was Bill Silcock, a silversmith and secretary of the fishing club in the 1950's

presumably the rates were higher. I haven't found an equivalent pricing book for stamping as exists for burnishing. Generally speaking for those employed in the metal working processes, the traditional areas of male employment received more pay. I noted several people's wages for this same week and of those I noted no woman's reaches a £1 and no man's is less. For this week in the plated department there were 219 staff and the total wage bill was £325/8/5d. There were two other departments, Britannia Metal with 155 staff and a total wage bill of £205/1/7d and the Powder Flask Dept with 53 staff and a total wage bill of £64/9/10d. (2) There would most certainly have been other workpeople such as clerks as well as those who maintained the various buildings. There were also apprentices who do not appear to be on the list. My own great grandfather as mentioned elsewhere became a silver stamper and he was, I assume apprenticed to his stepfather John Buxton. In March 1864 he was 17 years old. The workman to whom they were apprenticed probably paid the pittance that was the apprentices' wages. As noted in the chapter on apprenticeship, it was hardly generous nearly a century later when Barrie started work.

Looking through the archive material it is very striking how low the rate of inflation was up to the First World War. In 1916 some workers were receiving little more than the wages outlined above in 1864. The casters in the Britannia Metal Department seemed to be getting around £1/15/- a week, bricklayers £1/12/- and joiners £2/1-. I noted a couple of burnishers who earned around 15/-.

After the First World War the men in the plated department were earning more and there were huge differences between the different trades and in different weeks. The latter may well have been due to work available given how depressed the economy was. In 1918 whilst my grandfather Henry Cooper, a silversmith took home £2/19/5d net (5d having been deducted for

the salary received by other workers classed as 'staff'. Mr Constantine was works manager and Mr Deardon something like company secretary. His main areas of responsibility were to do with finance.

Calculating piecework

The pricing was either per item or per inch. For example the burnishing prices for the Spoon Department in 1864 are given as: *Fruit Spoons 380 6/- all over, 3/6d bowls only, 381 4/- all over, 2/-bowls only*. In contrast the price for meat dishes was 11/2d per inch. So for a 12" dish the burnisher would receive 1/6d and for an 18" meat dish 2/3d. There were similar ways of charging for tea and coffee sets with 4d extra if there was a sugar cover and 2d extra for a cream cover. (1)

Week ending March 11ᵗʰ 1864 my great great great grandmother Martha Barber earned as a burnisher at Dixon's 14/7d. Her daughter, Mary earned 16/1d and her lodger Ann Barker 17/9d. They lived at the time in St Phillips Row. My great great grandmother, Ann also a burnisher and by that time married for the second time to a John Buxton and living in Radford Street earned that same week 15/-. The discrepancy was to do with piecework rates. I assume that those earning more could work more quickly unless for some reason Martha worked less hours than her younger lodger. John Buxton. Ann's husband in the same week earned as a stamper £1/17/4d. Stamping was a male preserve so

TRADE MARK

60

income tax) his younger brother Harold a hollow-ware buffer earned £12/8/5d also having paid income tax. However in July of the same year both earned only 15/6d. (3) It is impossible to know whether this difference was due to one being datal and the other on piecework or whether one had apprentices and therefore a team and that this enabled him to earn a lot more. I believe that the latter was the case as there is a record dated December 1936 (4) in which Mr Constantine, the works manager, records that he was asked by a group of hollow-ware buffers to investigate:

1. more equal distribution of work
2. advantage obtained by C.Wallis owing to repair shops finding him work
3. that Harold Cooper got work for his girl which ought to be given to the men.

Mr Constantine writes 'I promised to investigate.' He says that he looked at wages over the past year and averaged them out per week. It transpired that Harold was earning more than twice as much as his nearest rival though he would have had to pay the girl out of that sum. The figures demonstrate the variations possible even for those paid at the same rates of pay.

Bagshaw 45/-
H.Cooper and girl 122/6d
Edwin Cooper (Harold's nephew) 50/6d
H.Copley 41/3d
G.Gabbitas 43/2d
F.Pidcock 39/10d
A.Spye 39/10d
C.Wallis 63/-
G.Wallis 53/-
F.Wragg 49/2d

Mr Constantine then sent for them. He continues 'all the buffers were present with the exception of A.Spye. I told them that C.Wallis would relinquish part of the new hollow-ware. With regard to H. Cooper discretion would be used when giving the work out to see that he did not get work for his girl which was not usually classed by us as girls' work. The buffers appeared to be satisfied with the arrangements'. There is a note. 'Later. Reported that all appear to be satisfied'

At the end of 1937 there were proposals to change from a five and a half day week to a five day week. It was decided, that such a move would cut running costs of having machines on for just 4 hours a day on Saturday. This involved a complicated rearrangement of hours to maintain pay at present levels for the same amount of work. They seemed to agree this between the different sections by cutting lunch hours and slightly lengthening the working day in order to get those Saturday hours into the other 5 days.

There can be no doubt that rates of pay and the whole issue of wages are extremely complex. This is confirmed by a paragraph in Pollard (5) in which he writes: *Wages in Sheffield light trades are difficult to estimate. Most men were paid by the piece, at rates bearing different discounts; in addition there were complications of deductions, rent payments, sub-contracts, the earnings of apprentices, the fluctuating volume of work available... Wages were normally on printed pricelists drawn up by the trade society alone or by agreement with employers. These pricelists were exceedingly complex, covering a wide variety of patterns and sizes, and included additional stipulations on the provision of tools, deductions and the like; some lists ran to forty closely printed pages. Price lists were therefore not revised very often: few lists survived less than ten years, and some remained in force for a century; temporary changes could be made in the form of percentage additions or discounts on ' list prices' or by altering the number of articles to the 'dozen'. Apart from reprints with minor adjustments, new lists would only be drawn up after major technical changes, or when a trade became strongly organised after a long period of weakness. Thus the pricelists of the first half of the nineteenth century were generally issued in years of boom and labour shortage; 1810 0r 1814, 1824-25, 1831, 1836 and 1844-46... In boom years, when wages were particularly high, hours were short, workman apparently preferring leisure to income after reaching their normal earnings.*

Sources

1 Sheffield Archives, Dixon's B535 Burnishers' Price Book
2 Sheffield Archives, Dixon's A250 wages paid by Ms James Dixon's to workpeople in their employ for the week ending March 11th 1864
3 Sheffield Archives, Dixon's A73 Minute Book 1844 ff.
4 Sheffield Archives, Dixon's A188 Volume marked S. Constantine random notes of some interest 1936-39.
5 Pollard Sydney, A History of Labour in Sheffield, Liverpool University Press 1959. p.59

Quality Pieces

During the years of the firm's existence many pieces were commissioned and designed in-house and made in the factory. The range of such goods that we actually know about was world wide and covered hugely different events and occasions. Some of these pieces were for individuals or families, including the Dixon and Fawcett families themselves, some were for Sheffield dignitaries and local events whilst others were to commemorate national events and occasions. Many were for royalty and famous people and others for those who simply had the wealth to commission and purchase them. One of the early pieces was an epergne (the centre piece of a dinner table to hold fruit and flowers) made about 1846 to be presented to the first James Dixon on the occasion of his seventieth birthday. It is called the 'orrocks' epergne and cost 200 guineas. Absolutely nothing is known about the designer or the craftsmen who made it. It seems amazing that these incredible works of art can be sold simply under the maker's mark. They seem to me to be as much masterpieces as any painting of a great master that would now change hands for millions.

Charles Holliday

The great designer who spent all of his working life at Dixon's was Charles Holliday. He lived in Wadsley, where the parish church has a large memorial to James Willis Dixon. In a magazine article Charles Holliday is quoted as having said

no-body knows what hard work it is to come up with an idea. Perhaps doing the job is its own reward in someways. I always got a tremendous sense of fulfilment from creating a thing of beauty ,something which will last for ever. It was always a challenge and very satisfying to see it through...in the final analysis, a designer is only as good as the silversmiths and craftsman who take his drawing and produce the finished article.... Between us we produced some great treasures (1).

He went on to give an insight into how he worked as well as something of the inevitable conditions of working in what was a business with time constraints.

The problem is that the piece in question is always wanted in a hurry. An organisation will decide that they are going to put up a trophy or something, and they set the date on which it will be presented before the design has even been put on the drawing board. So from the outset the pressure is on. I always begin by thinking about what it is supposed to represent, where it is going to go. I find myself dwelling on the subject for hours, days sometimes weeks. In that sense one is working even when one seems to be relaxing or doing something else. I usually do hundreds of sketches before I'm satisfied, and, almost invariably, I've had to consult some reference book.

In 1948 he entered a National Design Competition with a set of cutlery spoons and forks in silver and won first prize. For a silver tea service he got the third prize (2) He designed a special silver tea-set for the British Industries fair at Wembley in 1951. The then Queen Elizabeth came round and liked the set so much that she bought one. The tea-sets sold very well after that. For Queen Elizabeth's silver jubilee in 1977 Harrod's commissioned a centrepiece. It was intended that it remain on show in the store for the rest of the year. It had not been there very long when an American came in and made them an offer they said they simply couldn't refuse.

Another Harrod's commission in 1973 was to design and make £90,000 worth of rosewater bowl and ewer sets in solid silver to sell for £450 the pair. This was to commemorate the bicentenary of the Sheffield and Birmingham assay offices. The ewer carried the Sheffield assay office mark and the bowl the Birmingham mark. The first pair went to the Cutler's company.

To commemorate the same event Charles designed and Tony Martin made a medallion to be incorporated into a silver tray to become part of the silver collection of the Cutler's company. This was the first piece to contain Sheffield's new hallmark of the rose that replaced the crown. (3) Sheffield Cathedral also owns some unique pieces of Dixon's silverware, a set that

*The first piece of gold to be marked with the bi-centenary letter 'E' at
the Cutlers Hall Luncheon, 24th July 1973. Designed by Charles Holliday*

Prize-winning Silver Tea service designed by Charles Holliday

TRADE MARK

63

*Silver Candelabrum, designed by Charles Holliday January 1974 presented by
the staff of Savoy Hotels Group to Lord & Lady Mayoress of London*

consists of an altar cross and candlesticks, a processional cross, a verger's mace and the arms dish. In addition Sir Peter Roberts commissioned as a gift to the Cathedral, a silver altar cross which was designed by Charles Holliday and made by the Dixon's silversmith Trevor Collins. In 1967 the Girl Guides of Yorkshire presented a 16 inch silver arms dish also to the Cathedral. The firm also made a collection for a new Jewish synagogue in Cardiff, again the silversmith was Trevor Collins and the chaser was Dick Axelby. The breast plate was worn and the mace carried as a part of ritual worship. An original design drawing exists of a piece that was to be presented to a member of the West Yorkshire Police for the bravest deed of the year. The central feature is the old blue glass lamp that used to hang outside every police station. (see colour picture later in book)

Christopher Dresser, a man considered to be the father of Industrial Design

Candelabrum

Many of these were used as commemorative pieces. There was a luncheon at the Cutler's Hall on July 24th 1973 to celebrate the bicentenary of the Sheffield assay office. Charles designed a candelabrum that was to be the first piece of gold to be marked with the bicentenary letter E. (see picture on previous page)

To mark the Silver Jubilee (1952-77) of Queen Elizabeth 2nd a sterling silver 5 light candelbrum was designed by Charles, made at Dixon's and given by the Sheffield Town Trustees to the City of Sheffield. (see picture over page)
In January 1974 the staff of the Savoy Hotels Group presented to Sir Hugh and Lady Wontner, Lord and Lady Mayoress of London a 5 light candelbrum to mark their year of office. (see opposite page)

The other item of which Charles Holliday designed many is that of the freedom casket. Those he could recall were made for the Emperor of Japan, the Presidents of France, Mexico, Rumania and Canada, the King and Queen of Afganistan and the British Prime Minister Harold Wilson. Dixon's also had associations with a designer whom on the world scene is more recognised than Charles Holliday and his name is Christopher Dresser.

Christopher Dresser

Christopher Dresser is sometimes thought of as the father of home furnishing design. He was involved in the 1880's in setting up a kind of complete artistic household furnishing consortium. It was called the Art Furnishers' Alliance and he was employed as the artistic director. It aimed to supply the modern middle class with all kinds of house-furnishing material, including carpets, wall hangings pottery, table glass, silversmith's wares and hardware and whatever is necessary to household requirements. Firms involved included Sanderson's wallpaper, Cope's lace curtains, Liberty and Co. Linthorpe Pottery and James Dixon and Sons. (4) Dresser designed pieces such as tea services and a replica is on display in the Sheffield winter garden galleries. Dresser acted as the sole arbiter of taste and this made the concern unique. It was not a financial success. This could have been due to his ill health at this time making it difficult for him to properly manage it. His designs may also have been too ahead of their time to be popular but did anticipate both the 'art nouveau' movement and the 'art deco'. He died in 1904. The very sleek lines of his designs were an obviously huge contrast to the ornate styles that characterised the Victorian household decoration. Several Dixon pieces, some lent by private collectors were displayed in the 2004 exhibition that was called 'Shock of the Old' because the styles so anticipate the Art Deco movement.

In 1994 a man went into London Auctioneers Phillips with a small silver-plated teapot which was about four and half inches high which he could remember playing with as a child and which had recently been found in a cupboard. It turned out that it had been designed by Christopher Dresser and made by Dixon's in

TRADE MARK

65

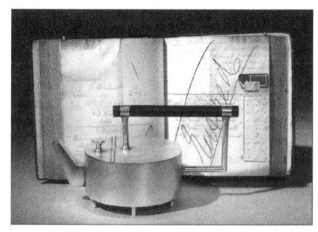

Teapot from 1879, sold in 1993 for £69,000 believed to be a costing prototype

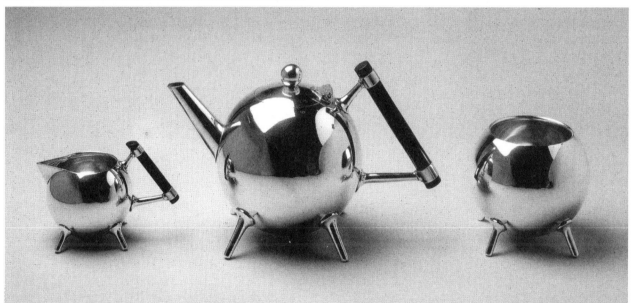

Silver tea set from 1880

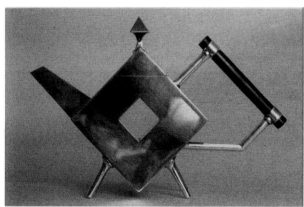

Christopher Dresser's designs made by Dixons. Some 37 designs were done by Dresser for Dixons, not all were made. Recently Sheffield Silversmith Brian Asquith has produced a number of designs for Alessi, the Italian tableware company. Sinclairs of Sheffield sell a reproduction on the above 1879 teapot, it retails for £7000!

Teapot from 1879, one of only six in existence it sold in July 2004 for just under £95,000

TRADE MARK

Sterling silver, five light candelabrum presented by Sheffield Town Trustees to H.M. Queen Elizabeth on the event of her Silver Jubilee in 1977. Designed by Charles Holliday, Silversmith Tony Martin

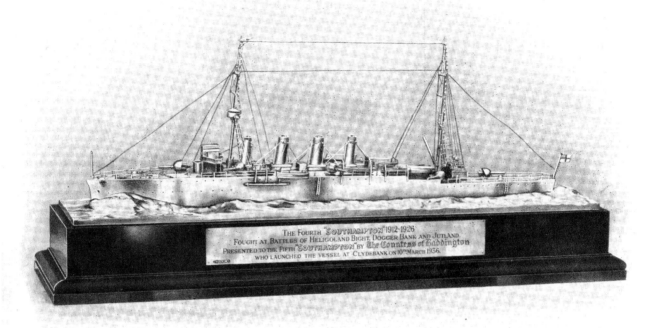

Model of the fourth H.M.S. Southampton which was presented to the fifth H.M.S. Southampton when completed on Clydebank in 1936. It is understood that this model remains on the Southampton, sunk near Malta in 1941 with the loss of 80 crew. The first H.M.S. Sheffield was a sister ship of the Southampton.

1879. Experts believe it was a 'one-off' made to work out how much such an item would cost on a larger scale. By coincidence, the calculation book detailing the cost of making the teapot was put up for sale by a different vendor. The costs were £1 5s 6d to make including 1 /- for the handle, 12s 6d for making and dressing, 3s 9d for metal and solder and 3s for polishing and turning. The teapot sold in the auction for £69,000(5). A similar calculation book containing other Dresser commissions is held by Sheffield Archives. (6)

There is a record in the works diary, I believe written by Sydney Constantine (7) in December 1951 where he records the receipt of a letter from the V&A museum in London. He writes: *A letter was received which mentioned an exhibition to be held next year and that they were anxious to trace the work designed by Christopher Dresser and to ask if he had at any time made designs for us. We were able to inform them that we had records of Christopher's Dressers designs and also a teapot made to his design. The records are in a PNS cost book. In connection with the letter which was of extreme interest to us, particularly seeing Dr. Dresser's teapot was so different to the types being made and sold at that period. Frankly the teapot has always during the last 40 years been the cause for amusement because of its unusual style. We await with interest further development.*

There must have been further developments because in 1973 Milo Dixon in an interview with a Sheffield Telegraph reporter commented on their small collection.(8) The article goes on to say: *What they have got is fascinating and if the Dr. Dresser teapot designed about 1889 is anything to go by, extremely valuable. Dixon's have more than once been asked to name their own price for the remarkable Dr. Dresser's brainchild which is constantly in demand for exhibitions at the Victoria and Albert Museum in London and other museums around the country. Defying verbal description the teapot looks as though it could as easily be dated 1979 as 1879.*

Christopher Dresser has very recently received a serious revival of interest so much so that in the spring of 2004 a major exhibition opened in New York at the Cooper-Hewitt, National Design Museum. This same exhibition transferred to the Victoria and Albert museum in the autumn of the same year. The Cooper-Hewitt's Director Paul Warwick Thompson said on the website 'Dresser is undoubtedly the most interesting of late-nineteenth century designers and the one whose work bears the most relevance to our present day concerns with production, form, materials and eclecticism. Dresser was instrumental in establishing the practice of working directly with manufacturers, employing new materials and machine processes, and creating inventive forms and designs to make affordable high

TRADE MARK

Award for bravest deed of the year,
West Yorkshire Police
Drawings by Charles Holliday

Above:
Charles
Holliday

Right: 1972
Grand National
Trophy won by
'Well To Do'

An elegant collection designed around 1830 in the time of William IV and displaying perfectly the grace and charm of that era.

Melon

902/1

Craftsmen in Sheffield Silver and Plate.

Drinks Measures

P1414 Wellington Boot   P4908

in Sheffield Silver and Plate.   MSC9

Collector's Market
I believe that some attempt was made in the 1960's to manufacture some products that were designed for people to buy as special gifts or as collector's items. Amongst these are the Bonbon dishes (see illustration), the drinks measures and the tea/coffee set called 'Melon', all of which I would describe as exquisite.

TRADE   MARK

quality products for a growing middle class. He was influenced by natural forms and plants as well as by Japanese art and aesthetics and after a visit to Japan and a book 'Japan: its Architecture, Art, and Art manufactures' he was responsible for fuelling in England a popular interest in all things Japanese. He also spent some time in America where he lectured and he was commissioned by Tiffany's to send back 'objets de art' from Japan.

Other pieces

Many of these were probably designed by Charles Holliday but there is limited information available usually written on the back of photographs. One world famous Sheffield Cutler is the firm of Joseph Rodger's. Their trademark is 'Vulcan' the Roman god who also appears on the Sheffield coat of arms. Dixon's made for Roger's small (about 3 inches high) silver statues of Vulcan which were presented to members of staff for long service. (see photograph). On the base was inscribed the name of the person to whom the presentation was made, the year, (in the one pictured 1944), and the name of the firm, Joseph Rodgers, also features.

There are records of pieces being commissioned such as in 1969 the University of Sheffield who wanted a silver centre piece and two candlesticks for the table to start off a silver collection. In 1960 a badge was made that was

to be worn by the Deputy Lord Mayor. This was in 9ct gold. (9)

One other discovery I have made is that the firm also did work that finished off as it were, pottery that is now recognised by the name of the potter. Classic among this ware is the William McIntyre/Moorcroft Florianware which features blue poppies. The small pots were 'topped' by an EPNS 'silver' band and in some instances had metal lids. All the metal parts were made by Dixon's.

Sources

1. Sheffield Assay Office Archives, Magazine 'Quality' 1982 Article by Keith Farnsworth 'Quality in the workshop'
2. Sheffield Archives Dixon's A199 Volume of Notes, memoranda marked matters of interest 1945-52
3. Sheffield Star Friday January 24th 1975
4. See www.achome.co.uk/movements/firms.
5. Daily Mail, Wednesday, March 30th 1994 page 5
6. Sheffield Archives Dixon's series B boxes 494 Calculation's Book 1878
7. Sheffield Archives Dixon's A199 Volume of Notes, memoranda marked matters of interest 1945-52
8. Sheffield Telegraph Saturday September 15th 1973
9. Sheffield Archives Dixon's A195 Volume marked 'Cash Book', but containing memoranda and notes 1952-62'

Made for Joseph Rogers to present to employees whom have served 50 years. It is their Vulcan tradenark

TRADE MARK

Relationships between the Dixon Family and the Workforce

The family firm

It is inevitable that in a society and culture where it was fairly common for people to spend their whole working lives with one firm and where son followed father into the same or similar employment that the sub-culture in such a firm would be very different from that experienced by most employees at the beginning of the twenty first century. Add to that, at management level, the son following the father into the family business so that virtually all the directors were family members and the dynamic within the whole organisation could not be more different than that generally existing today.

I am very sure that it had great weaknesses. At management level the son may not have had the talent or the skills of the father. The older generation may have resisted change from the younger generation when innovation might have been helpful to the development of the business. The whole thing could have been incestuous.

It also had strengths. Management would have an in depth knowledge of the business and of all the processes which were involved in production. Dick Axelby admired the fact that Milo had served an apprenticeship which involved spending time in each of the different sections of the factory and that he therefore understood just how the products were made. This meant that Dick had respect for Milo as 'the boss'. All though he says very little the feeling from listening to Dick is that this same respect didn't extend to the new management. Family pride would have contributed to maintaining quality of product and customer satisfaction. The firm's success was 'close to the heart' and the income.

In his book called 'Crashing Steel' (1), Stewart Dalton describes how the demise of the steel industry in Sheffield was in no small part due to the fact that after the replacement of 'family managers' through nationalisation and then acquisition by what we would call multinationals, businesses were increasingly run by those with accountancy backgrounds rather than by those who understand the products. Apparently shortly after one takeover, the entrepreneur Mr Jessel told the Observer that he had obtained the companies for 'bus tickets and used ones at that'. Dalton writes, 'that was exactly how it appeared to his employees. He cared little for steel, traditional values or indeed, even bus tickets'. There were certain processes where costs were cut that resulted in large quantities of products being eventually rendered useless or of inferior quality. He describes how 'So ill-versed were they with the *feel for steel* that usually the wrong questions were asked. In an effort to improve profit, by increasing output and reducing costs of preparing the slabs, it was decided to dispense altogether with the wrapping process. Of course experience indicated that the end result would be a failure but the old hands had learnt to let them get on with it so no notice would be taken of their advice anyway. The growing pile of very thin sheets-a result of the failure to weld together-was ample proof that nothing in the old, tried and tested method was done for the fun of it. The question that should have been asked was, could the same results of a well made iron and steel mould board be obtained by a different method? Management did not understand 'the business' only 'the bottom line'.

There are also some similar parallels drawn out by David Hare in his documentary play 'The Permanent Way' about the privatisation effects on the railways during the late 1990's to 2003. Questions are raised about the need for people who may well have high level 'management skills' to transfer between certain industries where people in management may also need in order to do the job effectively real in-depth knowledge of the specific industry.

There would in the past also have been quite longstanding relationships between staff and owners. Barrie once said to me 'I was a Cooper'. Everyone knew that there had been Coopers at Dixon's for generations. There are many stories that illustrate these relationships and in many ways I believe that one of the positive factors was the presence of trust. This is something often missing in the modern workplace. Balanced against this, the gap in income and

Sidney Constantine (works manager) standing right, Lennox Dixon (centre) with Mrs Florence Guy, aged 72, who had served with Dixon's as a burnisher for over 50 years, presents a silver tankard to retiring Lennox who also receives a wireless, December 1936

living conditions certainly in the first half of the nineteenth century was huge. I am sure also there was greater job security during the periods when the economy was stable. However the longstanding relationships could have made it difficult for management to 'lay-off' staff when economic depression came to the industry and obviously at those times economic insecurity was there albeit on different continuums for every-one.

It would also have been possible for there to have been the existence of 'collusion' between managers and workers in sticking with ways of doing things when it might have been time to ask questions. To ask the right questions though you have to understand all the implications of different possible answers.

In a family firm both management and workforce seemed to have commitment to the firm, a sense of pride in being part of the business and working together. There were occasional strikes involving the unions but these seem to have been very infrequent and on some occasions were supporting the union in action to do with other firms.

Today most of us are eager to leave the stresses and strains of the workplace, it seems there were many in Dixon's who wanted to stay on. There is a newspaper cutting (13th Oct. 1972 from either the Sheffield Telegraph or Star) in one of the books kept by Milo Dixon (2) about the retirement of Charlie Baxter of Walkley aged 90. He had worked for the firm for 77 years starting in 1895 when the hours were 6am to 8pm. He stressed that he was only retiring because his wife was not well!

The whole historical perspective is I am sure extremely complex, culturally, sociologically and materially and I do not want to romanticise this particular working context. There were drawbacks but there was also something quite unique about a family firm and some of the qualities such as trust and commitment that were present in a management and workforce have been lost and are big losses to the world of work.

Special relationships
Tucked in the back of one of the minute books is a small piece of paper that reads:

I Thomas Wolstenholme hereby promise to abstain from intoxicating liquors, to attend regularly and punctually to my work. Failing in the above there by agree that I shall be dismissed from my employment at the firm of James Dixon of Cornish Place Sheffield at a minute's notice. (23 rd May 1887 and witnessed by M.J.Hibberson). (3) I am not sure whether this was the same Thomas Wolstenholme who had written the first paragraph on the history of the firm at the beginning of the 1844 Minute Book (4) or another. However there is a sense of the firm trying to give to an employee a 'last chance'. Sadly I have been unable to discover for certain whether Thomas managed to abstain as promised. There is mentioned in a magazine article written in1919 a Thomas Wolstenholme who had 57 years service so perhaps he did. (5)

In Lennox Dixon's papers(6) there are copies of letters written in 1923 between Lennox and the Infirmary Hospital relating to the treatment or rather the lack of it of one of the employees. The woman, Mrs Clara Denton, was refused treatment under the '1d in the £1' scheme that I assume was some kind of early basic healthcare insurance. She apparently had no recommendation and was refused treatment by the hall porter because she didn't have a recommendation. She was later admitted as a serious case presumably after Lennox's intervention. In his letter to a Mr S.R. Lamb of Sheffield Joint Hospitals Council, he writes: *It seems to me that the first consideration of the Royal Infirmary is the Infirmary and the second the 'Penny in the pound scheme', both most excellent institutions. What they appear not to give sufficient importance to is the case of unemployed persons and the necessitous poor and I am glad to hear that you propose to pursue the matter further.*

During the First World War when men either volunteered or later were conscripted in to the armed forces, it seems that each was told that they would have a job with the firm when the war was over. In Lennox's papers is a letter from a previous employee, Fred Hornsey writing from India in 1919.

In his letter he tells Lennox that his demobolisation was delayed because of fighting in Afganistan and that he is now in Calcutta. He writes to explain that he has decided to stay in India as he has got a job with an engineering firm, Barn and Co. at 4 times his pre-war salary.

He says because of the promise made by Lennox of a job after the war he wants to let him know the situation so that in the language of the army Lennox can 'strike me off your strength'. He goes on to say that if there is anything that he can do in India for either Lennox or indeed to help the firm to please get in touch with him. He intends to keep in touch with Mr Blackton who I think was probably Dixon's representative in India.

This letter seems to be evidence of a quality of respect in relationship between the Dixon's and their employees and is reiterated by a speech given by one of the employees at the victory and peace celebration in 1919. Ex-sergeant A.W. Toyne said that the returned soldiers appreciated ' immensely the kindness and good spirit shown them during the war and since their return, by Mr Dixon. Especially did they value the spirit and policy of the firm in saving their jobs for them and welcoming them back as employees'

There are some interesting notes in 1920 which I think are by Mr Constantine who was the works' manager (7). It was rare for a non-family member to become a director and I understand that he had risen through the ranks. He was not a popular man. The notes seem almost to be a work's diary kept by Mr Constantine during this period. Within them is a clear indication of the way in which the management were willing to listen to the workpeople and to respond fairly.

In January 1920 an interview took place between the writer, Mr Dixon and a JS Spencer who thought that because apprentice wages were fairly high, he would be out of pocket if he were to risk taking an apprentice on. The writer states 'Mr Dixon seeing Spencer's position expresses his wish to help him up to a certain point but not to the extent of being unfair to those men who have not boys. Also he does not want to make J.S.' case a precedent'. After hearing Mr. Dixon, J.S. agreed to take a boy subject to the boy suiting him and 'I undertake to do my best for him'. The writer then goes on to reflect that. *'my own opinion of the matter is this. As I am out to help those who help the firm and myself and the men as a whole are against taking boys I shall place work to those who take apprentices (which are absolutely necessary for the good of the trade) so that they shall not be losers, at the same time as avoiding being unjust to those who have a genuine reason for not taking on an apprentice.*

On February 2ⁿᵈ Mr Dixon tells J.S. and myself that the trade agree to a man with an apprentice having 55% approximately more work than one without.'

I see this as a piece of high quality communication between all involved with evidence of listening and responding in order to solve what is a joint problem.

This sense of listening to people is illustrated in an incident from the same source in 1916 when an employee is failing to fulfil his contract. The works manager drew in Mr 'James' (Dixon). James Breen had signed a contract in which he had agreed to roll metal at the rate of 10d per cwt. and to pay his own boy out of that sum. All metal was to be done to gauges as requested by the 'cutter out.' The rollers were to be kept in a good and smooth condition. James Breen claimed not to have signed the agreement, which presumably was an admission that he was not fulfilling it. After listening to him, Mr 'James' asked him to sign his name then compared the signatures and declared them to be the same. The works manager also reflected in his own recording of the incident that they looked it to him also. No further information is given on how the total issue was resolved.

Family stories reflect something of the mutual respect in which the staff and the Dixon family regarded one another. I understand that almost every day Mr. Fawcett would go 'and have a word' with Harry Cooper, my uncle and that on more than one occasion he invited Harry to his home in Ashford in the water in Derbyshire. Harry never accepted. I think that this was because he thought he would feel 'out of place'.

I understand that when Barrie was approaching his 21ˢᵗ birthday, Harry went to see Milo Dixon, then a director and told him that he wanted to buy Barrie a really good watch for his coming of age. Milo sent to goldsmiths in London and got a selection of 4 watches from which Harry chose one. Barrie still has it and it works perfectly to-day, never having had anything done to it, though he does say he never wore it for work.

My parents had several fruit and flower shops in Sheffield including one they took on in the 1950's in the Ranmoor/Fulwood area of Sheffield where the customer list read like the who's who of the Sheffield industrial scene. My mother remembered telling Milo Dixon's wife about her

family's longstanding connection with Dixon's. The following weekend Milo Dixon came in to the shop and reminisced about her father and uncle and cousins. She told me this story only weeks before she died then in her late 80's.

Long Service records
In the magazine article quoted from previously in this chapter, it is noted that in1919 that the total number of years service made by all employees currently working at Cornish Place is 10,216. Eighteen of these aggregate 976, an average of just over 54 years each and a third of these are women. 'Chatting with a representatives of the *Goldsmith's Review*, they gave the expression to the kindliest sentiments towards their employers and told many stories relating to the firm and its progress'. One of these was a women called Ann Barker aged 71 years who in 1864 was lodging with my great great great grandmother, Martha Barber in St Phillip's Row. She was amongst those who received compensation for loss of wages following the Sheffield Flood. She claimed in the interview with the magazine 'to have never stayed away'. A Mrs Gregory who had 63 years service and who worked for the founder claimed she had seen her masters succeed each other generation after generation and that 'they've all been good 'uns.'

A women's welfare supervisor was appointed in 1919 and this was considered by the magazine to be somewhat innovative.

This again though was characteristic as there was a scheme supported by the firm known as the Silversmith's Sick and Funeral society first established in 1811 with a rules book published in 1812. Honorary members included firms like Dixon's, Mappin and Webb and Walker and Hall. This was still going strong in the 1930's and seems to have continued until the establishment of the Welfare State after the Second World War. I believe my Uncle Edwin Cooper had some responsibility for this or a similar scheme in the 1950's

By the 1930's there was a long established practice of presenting employees who had worked for the firm for 50 years with a teapot. Mr Constantine records that in December 1936 Mrs E. Gregory, L.B. Dixon and Albert E. Bingham were presented with the customary teapot which brought the total presented to date to 51(9). By 1966 the teapot had become a wrist

at Dixon's. I believe there were four marriages in my own family. Peter Perry could think of at least six in his era including his own to Sylvia. Roger Atkin told me that his father Frank who was the hollow-ware manager met his mother on Dixon's playing fields at Fulwood. The photograph is believed to be the Dixon's Hockey Team, year uncertain. Roger's mother is Florence Shephard, her mother and grandmother worked at Dixon's.

Dixon's Hockey Team, Florence Shephard,
2nd left, back row

watch and Len Bec was presented with one having done 65 years with the firm. My uncle Harry had a gold watch for his 50 years service.

To celebrate the coronation of George V1th in 1937 each man was given 10/-, the women who were over 21 5/-, the girls who were 18-21 4/-, and the younger girls 2/6d.

In the same year the firm co-operated with the milk marketing board in what appears to be some kind of national campaign to improve the health of the nation by urging the workforce to drink more milk. A committee was formed to start the campaign off and eventually the canteen took charge. Though this strategy might have been counterproductive as the staff in November 1937 were not making much use of the sitting room because of the poor quality of the meals.

Whilst on the subject of relationships it is worth mentioning that many people met their spouses

The firm had playing fields at Fulwood that were part of the estate at Stumperlowe Hall. These included a football pitch as well as a hockey pitch and tennis courts. Each year there was an annual sports day. According to Dick Axelby it tended to be the 'staff' who played tennis but the fields were frequented by some of Dixon's courting couples. I guess in the summer it was somewhere to go. They were sold off for development before Milo's residence at Stumperlowe Hall.

Sources

1. Dalton Stewart, Crashing Steel, Wharncliffe 1999 p68 & p74
2. Sheffield Archives Dixon's B447 Papers of Milo Dixon
3. Sheffield archives. Dixon's A73 Minute Book 1844
4. Sheffield archives, Dixon's A73 Minute Book 1844
5. Magazine article James Dixon & sons, Sheffield in war and peace in the watchmaker, jeweller, silversmith and optician', Aug. 1919.
6. Sheffield Archives Dixon's A186 Correspondence of Lennox Dixon
7. Sheffield archives Dixon's A192 notebook containing extracts from
8. documents, notes,, abstracts from agreements, extracts covering 1896-1923
9. Sheffield Archives, Dixon's A188 Volume marked S. Constantine random notes of some interest 1936-39.

Stumperlowe Hall today

TRADE MARK

Stampers, Spinners, Silversmiths and the rest

Dick Axelby using his hammer which is described in this chapter

To those of us whose relationship with silverware has largely been that of the admirer of finished products, the complexity of the manufacturing process is a revelation. My first visit to the relatively small firm, of Perry and Glossop, left me feeling stunned at the range and variety of tools at the craftsman's disposal. The owner in his younger days had worked for Dixon's and for part of the time with Barrie's father, my Uncle Harry.

When I looked at the workbench and saw the variety of chisels and hammers to select from in order to fashion a piece, I realised something of the level of skill necessary to achieve the perfect product. This was true for several different stages in the production of the article. There are hammers of different weights, sizes and shaped heads, some that have spring in them and some that are more rigid. One small hammer belonging originally to a chaser called Dick Axelby was worn in the centre of the handle to a fraction of its' original thickness and had been bound by string to lengthen the life of the handle. It was thought to be at least a hundred years old. A chaser puts the intricate carved patterns onto a piece of silverware.

The very beginning of the process of producing a piece of hollow-ware or indeed a new set of flatware would be with the designers who at the beginning of the nineteenth century had a suite of apartments on the first floor adjoining the offices. Their designs once approved went to the modelling room where the prototype would be made from the design previously produced in the design department. Approved models are then handed over to the die-sinkers who make a copy of them in steel. The dies are cut out of solid blocks of steel and once made they become a part of the company's product range. The dies of any firm are worth many thousands of pounds. The die is the starting point of the actual production process whenever a customer places an order. Dixon's die shop can be seen to-day at Kelham Island Museum in Sheffield.

Stamping

Sheets of metal were taken by the stamp shop to begin the process of production. A magazine cutting amongst Milo Dixon's papers outlined this process for flatware. It described how blanks were stamped from base metal, as many as possible from a single flat sheet by placing top to tail and how the shape was formed from alternately stamping and annealing in a gas fired furnace. If the bend near the prongs 'is not very pronounced it has been designed for machine finishing'. (1)

Hollow-ware was also stamped which means that the pieces are cut out by the stamp machine to the exact shape of the blank using the cutting tool appropriate to the blank. The stamp would 'cut' the different parts of for example, a teapot, coffee pot or entrée dish into shape and would also stamp on the pattern. The stamp machine could be up to one ton in weight and be capable of producing a hundred tons of pressure. The stamp beds were always on the ground floor and were set into deep pits. These were filled with vibration absorbing materials with sufficient 'give' to prevent vibration damaging the machine. In some instances there was wood below this rather like part of a tree trunk. The success of the 'stamp' was judged by the sound so even in later years stampers didn't wear ear protection. My great grandfather Henry Cooper was a stamper and can be seen in the picture in the Centenary brochure of 1906 working the machine. His stepfather John Buxton was also a stamper as was William or Billy his son, Barrie's grandfather.

Spinning

An alternative to stamping is spinning. It is a

*Top left: stamping cutlery, middle: electroplating, bottom left: casting,
bottom right: buffing*

*Top right: Silversmith, centre: hammermen, bottom left spinner,
bottom right: engraver*

Bill Ashworth, metalsmith known as the 'Passman'
i.e. Quality Control

The silversmith's then take the pieces and fits them all together usually by soldering. Care has to be taken that the solder used matches the metal, not only for aesthetic reasons but because of assay quality consistency. My grandfather, also Henry Cooper was a silversmith and my mother remembered as a child that when he came home, any small pieces of silver caught in the 'turn-ups' of his trousers had to be carefully collected and returned to work the next day.

After buffing, described earlier, the product would be sent for plating, unless of course it was solid silver. The plating room consisted of large vats into which the product was dipped in order to get its' coat of silver. The silver is suspended in cyanide of potassium and when an electric current is passed through the vat some silver sticks. It goes to a second vat which deposits the silver more slowly and makes the product harder and brighter. It is finally handed over to the finishers and or burnishers.

Sources

1 Sheffield Archives Dixon's A447 Papers of Milo Dixon memoranda book 1962-73, article from Emgas Magazine Spring 1975.

Henry Cooper with the stamp

process used when dies cannot be used. When products are oval or circular or where rims are required the craftsmen take a sheet of metal which is fixed on to a machine working like a lathe and revolving at high speed. The sheet is placed over a wooden mould attached to the machine and whilst it revolves, it is worked until it takes on the required shape. These moulds are made from different woods such as sycamore, beech, box or lignum vita, which is the only wood in the world which is so dense it doesn't float. Such moulds in a firm's stock are worth many thousands of pounds. Sometimes the heat generated through this process causes some distortion and 'a hammer man' would put the article such as a tray on to an appropriate shaped base and hammer back to the flat surface required.

Specialist craftsman using a variety of tools with fine points and of different shapes would do any engraving or chasing at this stage. The products are often fixed into a wax mould to secure them whilst they are being worked on.

TRADE MARK

Trophies

In the earliest of Dixon's catalogues of 'off the shelf' products that I have seen, there were always a variety of cups, shields, medals and sculptures of sports people in action that could be purchased by clubs, and other institutions to be competed for in sporting competitions. I have seen models of athletes and footballers. Such items could also be specifically engraved with the name of the event and club. The catalogue included specimens of engravings, badges and lettering together with a note that 'engraving in order to secure good wear should be done during the process of manufacture and enamel ware can only be engraved during the manufacture'.

Speed on ships

Most people have a vague awareness of the Blue Riband Trophy for the fastest sea crossing of the Atlantic Ocean. The first steam powered crossing was in 1833 and took about 18 days by the Sirius. The Blue Riband was a creation of the transatlantic shipping companies in the 1860's for the publicity opportunities of owning the fastest ship. What most people don't know is that for several decades there was no trophy, simply a blue pennant in the top mast of the ship. Some of the fastest crossings were made over the years by ships such as the Great Western in 1838 which took about 15 days followed the Lusitania in 1894 the Mauretania in 1907, and the Bremen in 1929. Incidently Lennox Dixon in September 1919 had a letter from E. Hobden of the Barbour Silver Company in New York saying that he 'was pleased to hear that (Lennox) was sailing on November 11th for New York on the Mauritania'(1).

By the time they were into the twentieth century they were getting specific commissions for especially designed trophies made of silver or gold.

The most successful designer that Dixon's had was Charlie or Chas. Holliday who joined the firm in 1927. He was trained at Sheffield College of Art and a month after joining the firm his mentor died so he was on his own.

I have discovered that it is practically impossible to find out information about the history of the actual trophies that are presented to successful sports people. It seems that people never look at or think about who designed this trophy or whose craftsmanship brought it into existence. This is not a field in which to gain worldwide recognition as an artist however splendid or even well known the finished product.

The Blue Riband trophy was the brainchild of a wealthy 'self-made' man called Harold K. Hales who was the M.P. for Stoke on Trent and who incidentally, was the man on whom Arnold Bennett based the main character, Edward Henry Machin, of his novel *The Card*. As a young motor engineer Hales had three goals: to be in a position to save ten thousand pounds, to be an M.P. and to 'present a trophy which would serve as a stimulus to the craft of speed and mechanical perfection which I have loved so well' (2).

In 1932-3 he commissioned the making of the trophy which was designed by Charles Holliday, Dixon's in house designer and made by the firm's own silversmiths. I believe my grandfather who was a Dixon's silversmith had a hand in this as my mother remembered it being talked about over meals when she was still living at home. Hales gave certain specifications concerning size and sculptures. The trophy stands nearly four feet high on top of a green onyx plinth. Dick Axelby recalled that the firm was unable to find a big enough piece of onyx in England and that the piece that was finally used had to be imported especially from Italy.

The sculpted portion weighs 602 ounces of solid silver. Dominating the design scheme is a globe supported by two figures representing Victory. Additional seated figures included Father Neptune holding his trident with his wife Amphitrite nearby. On top are two figures representing speed overcoming the Atlantic and in Hales words 'urging forward a modern liner'. The Atlantic is represented in pale blue with the track routes picked out in red. The direction of the four winds is indicated by a quartet of sailing ships, similar to the ancient caravels of early Spanish and Portuguese explorers. On a girdle encircling the central globe are four enamelled panels with illustrations of four liners who had previously won the Blue Riband; Great Western, Mauretania, Normandie and Rex. The Americans valued the trophy at £750,000.

The trophy was a milestone in the career of Charles Holliday bringing him to the forefront of designers and also enhanced the reputation of Dixon's which was already recognised as a high class producer of silverware. In the Sheffield Weekly Gazette in 1991 there is a feature about Richard (Dick) Axelby who as an apprentice worked on this trophy. He was allowed to contribute to the waves on the sea. He thought that they allowed him to work on the waves, because if he made a mistake which he didn't, it would not show.

The trophy was about to be presented to the Rex in 1933 when the Normandie broke the record. The Queen Mary surpassed this in 1938 but Cunard refused to accept it saying they were more interested in safety than speed.

Richard Branston raised interest again in the 1980's as a part of the publicity campaign for his then new Virgin Airlines but his attempt was disallowed as he had refuelled 3 times. A flurry of attempts on the record followed. A hovercraft, Cat-Link V, now controversially holds the trophy. The crossing was achieved in 2 days, 20 hours, and 9 minutes at an average speed of 41.3 knots in July 1998.

In 1998 two replicas were produced for American museums and cost $40,000 each. I believe the original is currently at the American Merchant Marine Museum at King's Point.

In 1948 there was a big 'Pageant of Production' held in Sheffield that several local firms participated in and which was opened by Princess Margaret. For this event Dixon's borrowed back from Henry Priddack and Sons from Hanley the Blue Riband Trophy. This was returned by road after the exhibition. One can only imagine the insurance costs of such an exercise in to-day's world.

Golf
In the late 1950's another stunning commission was to design and make a trophy for the American Masters' Tournament held in Augusta Georgia. The specification was to produce to scale, in silver, a model of the clubhouse.
The finished trophy stood on a base measuring three feet and six inches. A loose band surrounding the plinth was 9'6" in length. Charles had to work from the measurements given and keep them to scale and from a set of photographs.

The weight is recorded as being just over 625 ounces of solid silver and the piece took 4 months to make. The silversmith was Trevor Collins. At the time he was 22 years old. The firm also produced 6 silver replicas of the trophy. The tournament 'trophy' which seems to be more recognised is the 'green jacket' and the winner does keep this for a year and also receives a sterling silver replica of the trophy made by Dixon's in 1959-60 as well as a gold medal. Their name is engraved onto a silver band around the base of the permanent trophy that always remains at the clubhouse in Augusta. This is all in addition to the rather substantial 'purse'. The photograph was taken when the finished work was on display at Cornish Place. It was sent to Liverpool to be shipped to America on December 3rd 1960. The writer of the firm's records said 'In general it can be said to be a first class piece of craftsmanship'. The same source also says that the BBC (Manchester) came and made a film on December 2nd which was shown that evening on the Northern news programme and it also made the radio news and newspapers such as the Yorkshire Post, Manchester Guardian, Liverpool

Clubhouse American Masters Golf Tournament, Augusta Georgia, chaser Dick Axelby

Echo, Scotsman and Sheffield Telegraph. Early in 1961 the firm was congratulated by the Chigago firm, Spanling(?) and Co who had placed the commission on behalf of the Golf Club for the splendid trophy. (3)

Dixon's were also responsible for other golfing trophies, including the 39½inch high world cup and the Eisenhower trophy. Barrie remembers finishing one of these working with his father. We believe it was the World Cup. He remembers that the height made it very difficult to handle. It weighed 453 troy ounces of solid silver according to notes in Milo Dixon's papers. (4) It was so large and heavy that one of them had to hold it to take the weight whilst the other worked the machine to get the perfect finish required. It was immensely heavy and one slip would have caused irreparable damage. To help their concentration they actually locked the workshop door so no one could interrupt them as they worked. In the firm there was a lot of interest in just how they were going to manage the job.

Trevor Collins the silversmith who made the American Masters Trophy as well as many Grand National trophies. This is the 1961 trophy won by Nicolaus Silver

The Eisenhower trophy was made in 1958 for an annual event suggested by President Eisenhower and was for amateurs who played for their country in teams of four though in 2002 this was reduced to three. The first event was at St.

Andrews but in succeeding years took place at different venues in different parts of the world.

TRADE MARK

The National winner from a back-street

LAWRENCE GILL

HARRY WEBSTER

HARRY COOPER

Mrs DORIS MOORE

TREVOR COLLINS

TOM MIDDLETON   ARTHUR STANIFORTH

Charles Holliday—his design won

RICHARD AXELBY

Express Staff Reporter

THIRTY ounces of gold and nearly three months of shaping, hammering and polishing by craftsmen have gone into the trophy for the Grand National winner.

The trophy began as five small sheets of gold in a back - street factory in Sheffield.

Now the £600 prize, to be presented on March 25, is on show in a Liverpool shop window.

The work was done in the Cornish - place factory of James Dixon and Sons, silversmiths since 1806. This is the fourth time in the last five years that the firm has won the job.

The man who produced the winning design — 53 - year - old Charles Holliday, of Walders-avenue, Sheffield—is designer of all the firm's work, including knives and forks.

For him this was more than just another job. In his book-lined office he said : "The competition for this job was pretty stiff. It's always a thrill to get the commission."

From Mr Holliday, who supervises the work through all its stages, the job went to the oldest man of the trophy pro-duction line, 83-year-old Tom Middleton, of Rock-street.

Tom, 70 years with the firm, is the caster who made the model horses on top of the cup by pouring molten gold into moulds he made himself.

Lawrence Gill, 52, of Mont-gomery-terrace road, Sheffield, spun the cup into shape.

Next came 47-year-old Richard Axelbury, for Forres-road, Shef-field. He's the man who puts the ornamenation on the cup.

Says Dick : "The nicest thing about this job is that you never finish learning."

Burly Harry Webster, 70, of Edgedale-road, Sheffield, then

AND A WOMAN IS CALLED IN TO PROVIDE A SPOT OF BEAUTY TREATMENT

took over. He's the buffer. On his machine he gives that gleaming gold its first silky finish. The trick with his job is to make sure too many tiny particles of gold are not sheared off.

Harry Cooper, 53, of Dykes-lane, Sheffield, put more glitter into the cup on his polishing machine.

The woman in the team, 60-year-old Mrs Doris Moore, of Harold-street, Sheffield, her bare hands smeared in jeweller's rouge, gave the trophy its final perfect sparkle.

Mrs Cooper's hands are soft although she reckons she has

polished millions of articles in the job she has done since she left school.

The words "Grand National Steeplechase 1961" were put on the cup by Arthur Staniforth.

The youngest man in the production line had been doing things at all stages of the work but his main job was to assemble all the parts into the finished article. He's 23-year-old silver-smith Trevor Collins, like Mr Holliday, a College of Art graduate.

And now the trophy has gone the big question is : Will it go to Russia ?

ON

1965

M ORIO SHIGEMATSU looks hurt as he tries to lift the 60lb. trophy after winning the Windsor to Chiswick marathon in the world record time of 2hr. 12min.

The dilemma of the long distance runner

I don't blame him. I'd feel hurt, too. Morio came a long way—12,000 miles —and ran a long way—26 miles and 385 yards—and he left London yesterday for home with nothing.

After his great run a friend carried the trophy from the field for the little clockwork runner.

Then Polytechnic officials explained: "It can't be taken out of the country to Japan to show your friends . . . but you can leave it at the Japanese Embassy until next year's marathon."

So Morio couldn't take the trophy home, nor even the first prize.

Arthur Winter of Polytechnic Harriers explained

why. "I'm afraid we bought all Japanese prizes, radio set, camera, wristlet watch . . . but this was before we knew that three of the first four runners would be Japanese.

"They wanted something typically British so we will send them something on . . . something like Scottish rugs."

World Golf Cup, 39½" high

In the pattern books were a variety of presentation and challenge cups from which organisations could select something for their purposes. Each had a pattern number and would be engraved with the name of the organisation and the event. This was done as a part of the production process. This was far less expensive than a special design.

No. D 109

	Min.	1	2	3	4	6	8 pints.
Height ..	3¼	9	12	13¾	15	17	18¾ in.
Silver ..	£4 11 6	£15 17 6	£21 2 0	£29 8 0	£35 17 0	£50 0 0	£60 4 0
Plinth ..	6/6	9/6	10/6	12/6	15/-	17/6	19/-
Weight ..	3·00 oz.	17·00 oz.	24·00 oz.	36·50 oz.	43·00 oz.	68·50 oz.	82·50 oz.

Ghana Football Cup which was 'off the shelf'

The trophy was also about a metre in height. The chasing work was done by Dick Axelby and John Roddis and the decorations were leaves and full flutes. The designer was Charles Holliday, the caster Tommy Middleton, the silversmith Fred Sheperd, the buffer Harry Webster, the finisher, Harry Cooper and the polisher Doris Moore.

The Grand National

The other sport that has gained a lot from the expertise of designer Charles Holliday and the many unnamed craftsmen of Dixon's is the sport of kings, horse racing. In 1957 he designed the first of his Grand National trophies. He recalled that 'Mrs. Topham was the owner of the course in those days and I took the trouble to find out the kind of styles she liked...she also told me that I was the only designer who seemed to know the right way up to put the horse shoes' (5). Each year the Liverpool jewellers Boodle and Winthorpe invited tenders and designs. Only once in 17 years did Charles fail to provide the winning design. Everyone was made in 9ct gold. On March 7th 1961 the trophy for that year was shown on BBC television news. Boodle and Winthorpe wrote 'Please extend our congratulations to Mr Holliday and the craftsman concerned. They have made a wonderful job.'

The Marathon

In 1965, the firm produced a model of a runner in gold for the Windsor to Chiswick marathon. It weighed 60 ounces and the Japanese winner Morio Shigematsu was too worn out to lift it! The event was spnsored by Polytechnic Harriers who were very unhappy with the trophy design. The designer was in fact Constance Ann Parker, not a member of Dixon's staff. The problem was that the runner in the trophy was of entirely the wrong build for a marathon runner.

Football

It is recorded in March 1959 that an order was placed on behalf of the Ghana Football Association for pattern D109 in 9 ct. gold with a figure of a footballer on the cover. The figure was fitted into a lock up oak case. An engraved inscription appeared on the cup and the weight was 31.50 ounces.(3)

Contributions to other sports

Another trophy mentioned in Milo Dixon's papers is the Japanese Ambassador's trophy for judo but no detail is given. I have seen pictures in a private collection of a swimming trophy made for the 1967 Northern Championships and of the trophy for the European boxing championship, the trophy having at its pinnacle a pair of boxing gloves.

Sources

1   Sheffield Archives Dixon's A186 Correspondence of Lennox Dixon
2   Ocean Liner Gazette First Voyage article Winter/Fall 1998 found on www.oceanliner.org/hales_trophy.htm
3   Sheffield Archives Dixon's A195 Volume marked 'Cash Book', but containing memoranda and notes 1952-62'
4   Sheffield Assay Office Archives, Magazine 'Quality' 1982 Article by Keith Farnsworth 'Quality in the workshop'
5   Sheffield Archives, Dixon's B447 Papers of Milo Dixon 1962-75 incl.
6   Sheffield Archives, Dixon's B447 Papers of Milo Dixon 1962-75 incl.

The Harold Fern National Swimming Trophy, designed by Charles Holliday, the silversmith was Trevor Collins and the chaser Dick Axelby. Harold Fern was a major influence in the development of the Amateur Swimming Association, there were a number of trophies bearing his name.

TRADE MARK

Unions

Trade unions were a development of the eighteenth century. They usually began as some kind of friendly benefit society and graduated to looking after the working conditions and pay of members. In the cutlery and silver trades their development in Sheffield was complex partly because of the powers until 1814 held by the Company of Cutlers in Hallamshire. In 1814 together with other Elizabethan labour legislation the Cutlers' Company powers of regulation were ended and masters were free to train and employ as many men as they chose to. Remembering that Dixon's began in 1806 this landmark is significant though was not particularly recognised as such at the time.

I personally believe that this was partly due to the nature of the cutlery and silver trades where the different processes required very high levels of skill which in some ways separated out the various craftsmen into the culture known locally as 'little mesters'. This gave people the self-employed 'feel' so that the unions remained more as friendly societies with small numbers negotiating prices for jobs between themselves and who were in fact 'equals' but who specialised in different skills such as hafting or grinding. They owned their own tools, worked in a small workshop or even at home.

I recall Barrie saying to me in passing, relatively recently, that even though he was an employee of Dixon's, because he was on 'piece-work' he felt as though he was his own boss and he liked piece-work for that reason. It gave him some sense of independence which he valued. He was someone who was working in the relatively large established firm of Dixon's at a time when the Trade Union movement nationally was moving into one of its' most influential periods in the history of British Industry and in other industries was resisting any suggestion of 'piece-work' and using its' muscle to make some very heavy demands on employers. This was particularly true in the heavy metal industries such as shipbuilding and motor vehicle production as well in the iron and steel and engineering industries in Sheffield.

Steampower and Industrialisation

One of the industrial developments that contributed substantially to a shift from the 'little mester' model of working was the invention of steam power. In Sheffield at least the workers prior to the use of steam power had lived in rural contexts not too far from local water-powered mills. Dixon's is a good example of a larger concern using steam power in the early 1800's which led to workers becoming more town dwellers. They are also an example which was rare even as late as the 1850's of a firm who built a reputation on their trade mark and this was something to do with the rather more sophisticated techniques required to produce silver plated goods than was required in ordinary cutlery manufacture. Generally speaking though this was still unusual and the network of small producers who were inter-dependent still surrounded the larger concerns and the culture never really disappeared so much so that when by the end of the twentieth century these larger firms were scaling down or disappearing, some workers at least were able to return to the 'little mester' model of working and a very few still survive to-day in 2004.

I would like to be able to chronicle the relationship between the unions and Dixon's as employers but insufficient material as far as I know exists so what is available simply gives small glimpses of the relationship in different decades.

National Union of Gold, Silver and Allied Trades.

In the period between 1900 and World War 1 some of the small groupings of 'unions' connected to the light metal trades combined with similar groupings in Birmingham and London to form the National Union of Gold, Silver and Allied Trades.

The most influential person in this was a man called William Kean who began his task in 1903 by trying to bring together the separate Sheffield groupings By 1907 he achieved the amalgamation of the Sheffield and Birmingham Britannia Metalsmiths.

Prior to this the Britannia Metalsmiths' Provident Society had existed and in November 1898 had issued the following:

This meeting of the Britannia Metalworkers hereby instruct their members not to sign any agreement or otherwise consent either individually or collectively, to allow deductions from their wages for any reason whatsoever as it has come to our knowledge that such deductions are illegal, and further, that the decision above referred to, be communicated to each firm in the trade where deductions have in the past been made. Signed Wm. Day, Secretary, 44 Grimesthorpe Rd.

I have already outlined in the section on Apprenticeship something of what I believe was one of the most turbulent periods in industrial relations around 1900 and which was focused on the issue of the terms and conditions under which qualified workers would take on apprentices. In the section on pay I have looked at some of the union involvement that led to the establishment of piece work rates. I believe that this was probably the work of this same Provident Society. Certainly things seem to have settled by the time Kean was beginning to try to bring interests together in 1903.

In 1910 Keans began a series of meetings in Sheffield, London and later Birmingham and Dublin which led in 1911 to the formation of the National Union of Gold, Silver and Allied Trades. This was a significant achievement for Keans and he became the first general secretary. It seems that he was successful in not only bringing them together but also in welding them into a 'union'. He held office until 1953 and in 1934 was President of the Trade Union's Council of which he was a member for twenty years. When the Union was formed it had capital of £1952/10/10d and in 1919 a membership of 14,326 which by 1961 had shrunk to about 3,000. The office was in Sheffield in Trippet Lane and later in Kean Chambers in Mappin Street. This grouping negotiated rates of pay with approximate parity in different firms, conditions of apprenticeship and working conditions generally. Usually though they negotiated rates of pay for different 'crafts' within the industry and often these were piece-work agreements. (see chapter on 'Pay').

These fifty years of Keans' leadership were hugely difficult times for employers and for workpeople. These trades were hit very badly during the depression between the wars and the Union paid out thousands of pounds in unemployment benefit and industrial relations were also very difficult.

The relationship between the Union and Dixon's seems on the whole to have been a fairly healthy one. In 1931 one of Dixon's directors wrote that 'the present (union) officials are reasonable and are out for the good of the trade generally...cooperation is being urged in all trades'. (3) However given that between 1929 and 1932 the American Economy shrank by 40% with devasting effect on Europe and that international trade was in total confusion following the first world war so that in 1930 unemployment in Britain jumped by almost a million the unions were not in a strong position. (4) Sheffield was particularly bad. In 1932 the local unemployment figures were 34.1% of the population compared to 21.9% nationally. Cutlery had 42.7% and silverware 33%(5)

Once firms like Dixon's became established and began to take on increasing numbers of employees there was less tendency to, in modern terminology outsource work. Towards the end of the nineteenth and the beginning of the twentieth century it became a practice which was unhelpful to many work people and also to the maintenance of quality standards. This included those who were represented by a developing trade union movement but also the employers.

In good years, the in worker found it difficult to increase his earnings because of long term contracts and rigid piece price lists. In depressions he did relatively well since it was to the advantage of the manufacturer who kept a proportion of wages as rent to give him as much work as possible. At such times the outworker did very badly. The manufacturer spread the work around as many as possible where they were renting space from him in order to keep their rents. This pressured the 'little mester' into cost cutting which reduced not only his own income but that of any of his workers as well. He therefore ended up with the least skilled workers. Such concerns were also dependent on 'factors'. These men were the entrepreneurs of the age and who were probably in many instances fairly unscrupulous in their 'deals'. Pollard claims that, "Trade unions and manufacturers were united in opposition to the 'little mester' and the factor. Trade union rule books abound in prohibitions of the employment of datal men, of 'team work' and the sale of semi-finished goods by workman, and many encourage the practice of one month's notice"(6)

A particular dispute

In January 1926 Kean accused Dixon's of violating the agreement between the Union and the firm by the reduction of base prices and by making further demands for alteration of rates. In addition, there were issues relating to the amalgamation of Dixon's with Huttons as there is a record in one of the notebooks which reads ' An action by the Union for compensation for men thrown out of work by the amalgamation of Messrs Hutton and Sons with James Dixon's and Sons was satisfactorily settled out of court after considerable negotiations' (7)

Increasing benefits

In the 1930's there was correspondence between Lennox and other managers of other metalworking firms. Unfortunately there are the letters but not always Lennox's response. A letter from a director of Thomas Bradbury to Lennox says,

' *we ought not to loose sight of the fact that since the bonus was fixed at 45% there have been several social advantages given to the workman...old age and widow's pensions, health insurance, free meals and dentristry for children, extended tramway facilities...which amount practically to an advance in workman's wages but all this is never taken into consideration when we have these discussions.*

In a later letter from the same source the writer expressed the view that if Kean wanted firms to not give bonuses to non-union men that he on his part should undertake to withdraw all union labour from firms who are not members of our association, presumably the Master Silversmith's association. (8)

I particularly noticed a letter with an unreadable signature from some-one at the firm of John Turner's in which the writer says:

'*I presume you would support Alderman Blanchard in his effort to unify the forces against Socialism*'. (9)

I suspect we would read 'socialism' in this 1930's

context as 'communism'. Sadly there is no record of Lennox' response.

There does on the whole seem to have been a fairly cooperative spirit between the union and the various firms. Dixon's was very influential though the background of two world wars and an acute depression needs to be seen as a context. In the short history written for its' 50 year anniversary the union writer said 'although a major dispute has often seemed likely it is only on a few occasions that any labour has had to be withdrawn'(10)

Sources

1   Pollard Sidney. History of Labour in Sheffield Liverpool University Press 1959 p.57
2   Sheffield Local Studies library, Local Pamphlets vol 225 No14 A Short History of the National Union of Gold, Silver and allied trades to commerate the 50th anniversary of the Union 1911-1961
3   Sheffield Archives Dixon's A192 Notebook containing extracts from documents, notes, memoranda etc, 1896
4   Fraser Rebecca, A popular history of Britain Chatto and Windus London, 2003 p.686
5   Binfield C. et al (ed) The history of the City of Sheffield 1843-1993 Vol 2 Pollard Sydney, Labour, Sheffield Academic Press, p.273
6   Op cit Sheffield Archives A192
7   Ibid
8   Ibid
9   Ibid
10 Op Cit Local pamphlets vol 225 No 14 p.8

TRADE ☙ MARK

Visitors

The firm obviously had visitors associated with the industry who came to see the products on offer at the showrooms. However it did on occasions have special visitors. Some of these were in Sheffield for other purposes and Dixon's would be one of the firms chosen for a visit.

Prince Leopold

The first of these on record is that of the youngest of Queen Victoria's sons, Prince Leopold who came to Sheffield in 1879 to open Firth College. He was a guest of Mark Firth and was entertained by him at a ball held at the Cutler's Hall and also at the works of Thomas Firth and Sons in Saville Street. The visit is commemorated in that one of the city centre streets is named after the Prince, Leopold Street. He also visited James Dixon's. The local paper (1) described the visit: *There is probably no establishment in the world where His Royal Highness could have seen the manufacture of silver and silver plated goods conducted on a more extensive scale or to greater perfection than at the works of Messrs James Dixon and Sons, Cornish Place...where men and women were manipulating the most precious of metals with true artistic skill into articles of the most exquisitely beautiful form and design.*

He visited the steam stamp shop where he witnessed the stamping of spoons, forks and all kinds of hollow-ware. He later watched the process of pressing patterns on to articles such as silver salvers where to the untrained eye it is impossible to tell a stamped article from an engraved one. The stamp could apply the slightest pressure or as much as 100 tons. I wonder if my great grandfather met him? He was a Dixon's stamper and would have been 31 years old at the time of the visit.

He was presented with a silver p? and salver each of which was engraved with the Prince's coronet and monogram. The Prince was never very robust and suffered from haemophilia.

The Shah of Persia

The Shar of Persia was another noted visitor. However he seemed to lack the staying power of British royalty and was running late all the second day of his visit as he had found the first so exhausting. On his arrival at Cornish Place he was greeted by a yard full of flowers which had come from the gardens of the workforce. The Independent's reporter found this amazing: *it told of a widespread love of flowers hardly to be expected amid a toiling industrial community and of hearty co-operation and mutual goodwill between employers and employed... Every window-ledge on the ground floor had an attractive array of pot flowers before it while here and there blank wall spaces were broken by brilliant banks of flowers which would have done credit to many horticultural exhibitions.* Actually my Uncle Harry right up until his death in his 90's (a Dixon's finisher) was still taking cuttings from flowers which he had brought from his grandfather's garden in Hawthorn Rd when he was married in the 1930's.

The Shar was presented with silver engraved pocket flask in a richly lined velvet case in memory of his visit. He also made several purchases and was particularly interested in a self-pouring teapot which was a Dixon's speciality. He signed the visitors' book along with his son and also the Duke of Norfolk and other accompanying visitors but didn't do the expected tour of the works. The employees were very disappointed but the Dixon family and others who were in attendance did this instead.

Lord Kitchener

A later visitor was Lord Kitchener who was in Sheffield to receive the freedom of the City 'in recognition of his eminent services rendered to the country' (3)

The great connection with Sheffield was really through the armaments industry, and he made reference to Vickers. He said that he 'was able conscientiously to give the order to a great firm now established in Sheffield' that was to rearm the Egyptian army. However the presentation made to him by the city consisted of a service of silver plate and a case of cutlery, 'every article of the best workmanship'.

The service of silver had been made at James Dixon's and consisted of 30 soup plates and 60 dinner plates and weighed about 2,000 ounces. According to the Independent ' these were of the type made in the reign of the Georges. 'The plates both soup and dinner-are ten and three quarter inches diameter. The chaste border is formed of four beautifully fluted and beaded shells with richly matted terminals and four fluted and matted shells with plain terminals, placed alternately, the whole being connected by a combination of leaf and words. 'City Of Sheffield' are engraved under the principal centre in the inner flange of the plate and Viscount Kitchener's Arms with supporters opposite. The whole of the service is placed in a handsome and massive cabinet of oak, one of the drawers being made to contain Viscount Kitchener's burgess ticket. On the right hand door the Arms of Viscount Kitchener are carved in bold relief, the arms of the city being carved in a similar manner on the left hand door. A silver plate is fixed on the cabinet, bearing the following inscription:-*Presented together with Honorary Freedom of the City of Sheffield, to General Viscount Kitchener of Khartoum, of the Vaal, and of Aspall, G.C.B., G.C.M.G., and O.M., by the Corporation of Sheffield, 30th September 1902'*

He was also given a canteen of cutlery made by Mappin and Webb.

When he visited the works of James Dixon and Sons he saw both the electroplating and silver plating processes and was given 'a handsome silver flask, decorated with his coat of arms and also a waiter to match the service of plate presented to him at the town hall'

When he thanked the City after the presentation at the town hall Lord Kitchener said that the gifts 'would be of great practical value to him in his new position as Commander-in-Chief in India!'

The Japenese Ambassador

In November 1966 His Excellency the Japanese Ambassador Shigenobu Shima visited Cornish Place and then had luncheon at the Town hall with the Lord Mayor, Lionel Farris. This was a return visit for the dinner he gave to Mr Dixon as President of the UKCSMA and the 4 members who went to Japan to arrange a quota for spoons, forks and knives. (4)

The BBC

A little known fact is that there was on one occasion a visit from the BBC. This was in November 1936. Mr. Constantine (5) the works manager notes that 'Mr Smythe brought their recording van to make a record of the singing (whilst at work) by a shop (Charlie Baxter's) of

buffer girls. This record was made for broadcasting purposes and the same will be on air early in the New Year.'

Further Royal connections

Although they never visited the works, Mr Constantine does report that at the 1938 British Industries Fair at Olympia, 'our stand was honoured by a visit from their majesties Queen Elizabeth and Queen Mary. Certain purchases were made by them.'

Imperial Defence College

Mr Constantine records in 1951 the visit of a group of high-ranking officers from the above institution. These included a Brigadier, Major and an Air commodore. Each was presented with a souvenir flask to commemorate their visit, the reason for which is not stated. (6)

Midwives.

It is recorded that on September 15th 1961 24 members of the midwives association visited the works. (7). I assume this was some kind of 'outing' as I can see no link at all between Dixon's and midwives!

Sources

1. Sheffield and Rotherham Independent October 27th 1879
2. Sheffield and Rotherham Independent July 15th 1889
3. Sheffield and Rotherham Independent October 1st 1902
4. Sheffield Archives, Dixon's B447 Papers of Milo Dixon c.1962-73 incl. memoranda book.
5. Sheffield Archives, Dixon's A188 Volume marked S. Constantine random notes of some interest 1936-39.
6. Sheffield Archives Dixon's A199 Volume of notes and memoranda marked matters of interest 1945-52.
7. Sheffield Archives Dixon's A195 Volume marked 'Cash Book', but containing memoranda and notes 1952-62'

Main gate from the inside yard, time keeper's office on the left.

Warehouse and Showrooms

The warehouse stored both completed goods and partly finished goods and was mostly staffed by women workers. In one of the books in the Sheffield Archives (1) there is a loose page in the section dated 1898. This is a handwritten notice obviously intended for posting on a notice board. It has the same 'feel' as notices posted on the staff room notice board in my early days as a teacher in the 1960's. It is in essence stating the expected procedure for the women to follow, particularly in relation to working hours.

Showroom 1906

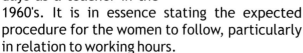
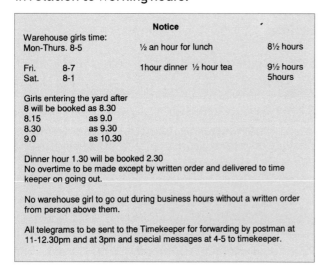

Notice		
Warehouse girls time:		
Mon-Thurs. 8-5	½ an hour for lunch	8½ hours
Fri. 8-7	1hour dinner ½ hour tea	9½ hours
Sat. 8-1		5hours

Girls entering the yard after
8 will be booked as 8.30
8.15 as 9.0
8.30 as 9.30
9.0 as 10.30

Dinner hour 1.30 will be booked 2.30
No overtime to be made except by written order and delivered to time keeper on going out.

No warehouse girl to go out during business hours without a written order from person above them.

All telegrams to be sent to the Timekeeper for forwarding by postman at 11-12.30pm and at 3pm and special messages at 4-5 to timekeeper.

The original is handwritten

There is one very interesting document dated Oct 28th 1937 in the archives written on the firm's headed paper. It is a kind of report on the state of the warehouse. However it has the feel of being written on the initiative of those who worked there rather than being a report requested by the management.

It is as follows and I have attempted to use the punctuation and spelling as used in the original handwritten document:

Silver Dept-Warehouse
It is obvious that the lack of space retards efficient working. It must be remembered that the Department handles the most expensive materials used in the factory. It also produces the finest examples of work-manship. If one considers the seemingly muddled appearance of the room on any working day, the opinion must definitely be formed that more space is required. It may be argued that the space has sufficed in the past and ought to do so now the handling of the Hutton business means that many more patterns are always on the move and at present there is little room to even lay them preparatory to their next process. Two proposals-at little expense are open, to gain more space.

1st take in the Repair Room making a definite passage way so that the room obtained is actually part of the present Sil W'house.

? If any difficulty in removing the present dividing wall between the 2 rooms

2nd Flask Warehouse (Rather dark) a fairly big room, which by transferrence of the Bri & E.P. flasks to the present Sil. warehouse would enable the present Sil. Dept to be transferred there. It should be remembered that all silver goods other than finished factored goods, have their origin up to the polishing state and have to be handled by the Sil W'house.

The 2nd scheme has much in its favour, as apart from extra space gained, the doing away of silver hollow-ware (finished) being in two depts-all would be in one room- The savings in stocks would in my opinion be remarkable.

Again why is it necessary for orders to be dissected by the office when ultimately they will be re copied out for trans-ference to the

Sil. Dept. for production. Again why separate handlers?

In brief two rooms are carrying similar finished stocks, although one of them is responsible for the production for both. The scheme is a feasible one seeing that there is no clash departmentally and no drastic change of policy. The turnover in any case goes to the one Dept.

Points
All the material for the two sections is bought and handled by the Sil. W'house. All the production ditto. Both rooms carry stocks of cups, bowls, s.boats, inkstands, dredges, condiment sets, tea sets etc.

Lottie May Taylor, warehouse 1920's -30's. Married Harry Cooper, finisher

The diverting of an order containing what are known as B'ham goods (although made here) must mean that coordination of production cannot reasonably be assured, with those known as Dixon goods.

If scheme 1 was used there is difficulty of finding room for the Repair Dept. which must be in proximity to the lift and General office. Cannot think of a suitable substitute.

Scheme 2
C. Peat   A. Holden   G. Bramah
Alice   Sylvia   Ethel
Plus younger girls

I find this an interesting document in that here is a department finding working conditions almost impossible. They seem to have discussed it thoroughly amongst themselves in the warehouse and looked at it as a piece of problem solving. They were then prepared to put into writing a couple of suggestions to improve the situation which they believed, would lead to increased efficiency and a streamlining of production. This is against a background of a works' manager who had a reputation for being fairly unapproachable.

I have not so far been able to find the response he gave nor the outcome. I can only hope that they were taken seriously and that something positive came from it all. The management was at the time very preoccupied with moving the entire firm from a 5½ day week on to a 5 day week. We do have on record that the warehouse girls from each department welcomed the scheme.

Showrooms

There were showrooms in London as well as in Cornish Place. There are in the archives the folios (3) listing the stock to be found in both showrooms. The folios are about 12" wide and 15½ in length and very thick. All are obviously handwritten with lots of alterations and small pieces of paper stuck over numbers.

At Cornish House there were about 90 items for Silver Department which was A dept. Mostly there was 1 item from each product range though there could be up to 5. In January 1968 products listed at Cornish House included:

Silver jug (4)	weight	23.00	price	£46
Child's mug	"	4.75	"	£ 7/11/3
Snuff Box	"	2.40	"	£ 5/16/0
Waiter	"	28.90	"	£ 39/ 7/6

The total stock in the showroom from all departments amounted to £17,272/12/5d.

London

The story in London was similar. The showroom was in St. Andrews Street Holborn Circus. Here also items were listed by weight and price and included a silver kettle, silver marmalade pot-holder, a waiter and a flask. The total stock was priced at £16,850/11/1d. This was closed on Dec 31st 1967. In Milo Dixon's own copy of the product range book showrooms with an address are also listed in Melbourne and Sydney. In addition it lists without any addresses showrooms in Lausanne, Cape Town, Johannesburg and Durban.

Sources

1   Sheffield Archives Dixon A73 minute book dated 1844
2   Sheffield Archives Dixon A188 Volume marked S. Constantine random notes of some interest 1936-39. (Document loose inside book)
3   Sheffield Archives Dixon B104 Cornish House and London Showroom Stockbooks 1967-68 & 1965 respectively in one volume

TRADE MARK

Xylonite and Other
Knife Handle Materials

Steak knife and fork with horn handle

In the 1880's celluloid products such as xylonite, vulcanite, and ebonite became the more common products from which knife handles were made.

Xylonite was certainly increasingly used for making knife handles at Dixon's in the first decade of the twentieth century. Xylonite is a word originally coined by Daniel Spill as the trade name for his improved version of Alexander Parkes' Parkesine Material. 'Xylon' is the Greek word for wood. It is essentially a plastic and knife handles were one of its earliest uses but it was also used to make imitation coral jewellery as well as tubes and insulating materials for electric cables. It is variously described as fake ivory or celluloid ivory and some products from the art deco period are like bakelite, very collectable. Among these are things like napkin rings and playing card boxes. Most everyday knives were increasingly made from metal as the century moved on but even in the second half of the twentieth century xylonite was used for the handles of specialised eating implements for people with disabilities. One of its drawbacks was that it is very inflammable and Barrie remembers more than one fire in the workshop when this kind of material was being used.

In May 1938 Mr Constantine the works' manager complained about the rise in prices. Apparently all the suppliers increased prices by 2d per dozen on popular lines and 1d on the rest which

was a 12½% increase. Although he thought they could absorb the rise it was not very welcome at a time when the cutlery trade was doing so badly.

Prior to the invention of plastic products knife handles were made from natural resources which in the twentieth century were increasingly used for more luxury items or specialist products. As the century moved on these resources became more expensive and there were serious concerns relating to conservation and preservation.

Mother of Pearl
Such products included mother of pearl. There are several different varieties of mother of pearl harvested in different parts of the world. Pink freshwater pearl is found in the lakes of the Mid-Western United States and is a diminishing resource. It is now supplied in different grades and priced by the square inch. A nice matched pair of pink pearl 3"x1"x1/8" will cost about $65. In the Dixon catalogues it was usually used for serving implements such as fish servers or cake knives often with blades of silver though not always and usually boxed in a velvet-lined case.

Horn
Cutting implements such as meat knives or game carvers frequently had stag handles and sometimes horn. This type of material was usually carved often with deep lines running the length of the knife handle giving it a seriously rough look and feel. Different colours and textures were achieved depending on whether the interior or the exterior of the horn was used. This commodity was particularly desirable for hunting knives and those produced for other sporting or working contexts. In the 1908-11 catalogue is an engineer's pocket knife with magnifier, dividers and 'feelers' which has a staghorn handle. What is described as a sporting knife can be had in 'pressed' staghorn or in bone. The rugged look of the horn or bone no doubt enhanced the 'manly' image.

The horn industry is known to have existed in Sheffield since at least the seventeenth century but experienced rapid growth at the beginning of the nineteenth so that by 1850(1) there were 145 firms related to the horn trade employing 'well over 1000 hands'.

Ivory has been used for knife handles for centuries. An elephant actually appears on the coat of arms of the Cutlers Company and there are over 456 elephants in one form or another around the Cutler's Hall. The original wooden staff of the Beadle is topped with the emblem of the Cutlers and it is the elephant head which sits right on top. In the main room of the Master Cutler's Rooms is the oldest painting in the building dating from 1638. It has on it what is probably best descried as the artist's imaginative impression of an elephant. At the time he would have had very little to go on and would certainly never have seen one. (2) On a recent television programme industrial archaeologists were showing an elephant's tusk they had actually found in an underground storeroom. In 1938 there is a record of a rise in the price of ivory of 10% which meant that 6 pairs of fish eater handles would cost £34/1d.

Elephant Ivory has a very fine even grain and is easily carved in all directions. It can be thinly cut for the handle of a penknife and has the potential to be very delicately carved. In addition it can be painted, stained, dyed and gilded. When cut, the pores of the ivory fill with an oily substance, which helps the ivory polish up nicely. Because ivory has no blood vessel system it is denser than either bone or horn. It was usually elephant ivory that was used but walrus, sperm whales and hornbills as well as hippopotamus all have ivory tusks though each is structurally slightly different.

Hafting

In more recent years table knives were increasingly made with handles using the same substance as the blade. I.e. silver, EPNS or steel. Occasionally they might have been stamped all in one piece but the better quality product still had the handle fitted separately on to the tang. Generally speaking what is described as a full tang is a better quality product. This simply means that the tang, the piece of metal coming as a continuous piece from the blade is of sufficient length to run the full length of the implement handle. This means it is stronger than a half tang or any other kind of tang. High quality knives and other cutting implements have a 'full' tang as a marketing feature.

Fitting handles to tangs was one of the trade skills in the cutlery manufacturing business and

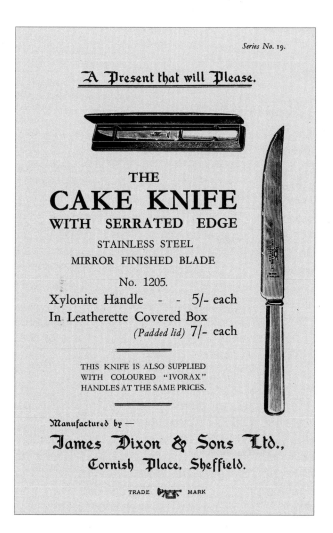

these workers were known as hafters. They had to be able to work with the different materials such as horn or bone and later in the development of cutting implements, plastics such as xylonite.

Sources

1 Beauchamp Victoria & Unwin Joan The Historical Archaeology of the Sheffield Cutlery and Tableware Industry 1750-1900, ARCHUS 2002 p.67
2 Beedham Ann, Peeks at the Past in Sheffield and Surrounding area, pub.2000 Pickard Publishing pp82-84
3 Sheffield Archives, Dixon's A188 Volume marked S.Constantine, random notes of some interest 1936-39

TRADE MARK

Yarns and Mysteries

Missing Person, Francis (Frank) Cooper, Silversmith,

In the family records is a marriage certificate for a Francis Cooper to an Ann Barber in August 1847. They were married by special licence in Dronfield. Two months later in November they had a son Henry who was my great grandfather. On the 1851 census return Ann is reported as widowed. I have never found a record of her husband Francis or Frank Cooper's death so I have my doubts but she did marry again some years later. Perhaps Frank deserted. Perhaps for Francis it was a case of 'marry in haste and repent at leisure'.

My mother, Mary Bell (nee Cooper 1915-2003) remembered her referred to as Grandma Buxton and that if she appeared in the street on a visit; everybody took cover, as she was a real 'battle-axe'. Was she like this around 1850 contributing to Francis' possible decision to leave or did she become like this as a result of his desertion and other difficult life experiences? An elderly Uncle Harry (also a Dixon's worker all his life) who died in 1999 when in his 90's knew of no family stories about Francis though Harry's brother was christened Frank. This may have some link to Francis who was known as Frank and who was his great grandfather. If you know anything of his whereabouts after 1851 please get in touch with the author!! I am very certain that he served his apprenticeship at Dixon's and very possibly he might have been apprenticed to his father in law who was also a silversmith. I know with absolute certainty that his mother in law, wife and sister in law all worked for Dixon's so it seems a very fair assumption that this is where he met his wife.

Fatal Accident

My great uncle and Barrie's grandfather was a silver stamper at Dixon's. Barrie knew from his father that there had been a fatal accident in the stamp shop sometime around the beginning of the World War 1. Apparently, William Cooper or Billy as he was known, left the stamp shop one lunch hour. On his return he found a colleague in the workshop who had been decapitated by his own machine. It seems that the man must have been leaning into the machine to do some

William (Billy) nearest Cooper in the stamp room around 1906

maintenance and the drop came down, rather like, I guess a guillotine.

Barrie understood that his grandfather never really recovered from the shock. Today we would expect and describe this as post-traumatic stress syndrome. He died before the end of the war officially of pneumonia. This experience came on top of the loss of his two small daughters just a few years earlier and within a couple of months of each other from scarlet fever. Anyone who has worked at Dixon's knows this story of the fatal accident in the stamp shop. I have not been able to find reference to this in the Dixon records and the coroner's office does not keep records that go back that far. If it did happen in World War 1 it may not have got into the newspapers but in any case no one seems to know the name of the man who was the tragic victim.

Princess Margaret and Lord Snowden

In the photographs that came from Dixon's when the firm closed is the one opposite of Princess Margaret and Lord Snowden being presented with what we think must be a canteen of cutlery made at Dixon's. There is no indication of the occasion or the event or of who the others in the photograph are. The date has to be after their marriage which was in 1960.

Princess Margaret and Lord Snowden

War memorials
On one or two of the photographs taken in the yard there is a war memorial recording those who lost their lives in World War 1. This was in position up until the time when the firm finally closed. However no one now seems to know where it went.

Similiarly a bronze plaque was designed by Charles Holliday and made by silversmith John Thorpe to record those who were in the services during World War 2. It also recorded the death in action of Spotswood R.N. It was handed to the ex serviceman's association, I think of the firm, after a dedication ceremony in which 60 of them paraded on Armistace Day in 1947.

TRADE MARK

The Occasion?

It seems as though it was fixed to the wall inside the building in one of the rooms. Incidently Barrie Cooper remembers this parade as an annual event. Does anyone know the answers to these mysteries?

A Portrait
On his retirement William Fredrick Dixon (2nd generation) was given a full length portrait of himself which for many years hung in Cornish Place. No-one seems to know what has happened to this. Another mystery.

Two Gatherings - What For?
The photograph on the right shows the war memorial on the wall but there is no certainty as to the reason for the gathering. It might be an armistice day service or simply a fire drill. Certainly a cool day as most are wearing coats.

This photograph shows what appears to be the workforce and staff sometime in the early twentieth century in the yard at Cornish Place. Anyone any ideas of the date or occasion? They seem to be dressed up and there is some special group of men or mostly men under cover at the back. This suggests whatever was happening occurred in the yard rather than simply being people gathering to go somewhere else. It looks fairly summery judging by the womens' light coloured dresses.

Yarns
In any family firm stories relating to the family are always retold. Dick Axelby recalls hearing that there was one occasion in the days of Lennox when he phoned the timekeeper to ask if his car was in the yard. The timekeeper replied 'No sir you arrived on foot this morning'. His chauffer driven car arrived shortly afterwards. Lennox had ordered the car and then gone and caught the tram and the chauffer had followed him down! Amazing that in the early 1930's the tram got there first.

Any Answers
If anyone does have any information which might throw more light on any of the above yarns ¯or mysteries, the author would be delighted to hear from you.

01636 816012   pbell7@btinternet.com

Zenith - When was it?

When trying to answer questions of evaluation it always depends on what criteria you are using. In our society to day we make such assessments mostly using numbers. Schools are judged on the number of exam passes, doctors on how many patients they see and so on. Less attention is given to assessing quality, simply because it is so much more difficult to evaluate whether a child has been stimulated to learn more by a teacher's skill as an educator or whether a doctor has made a patient feel listened to and valued.

Employees and Products
Using the criteria of number of staff employed the firm's zenith would have been around the beginning of the twentieth century up until World War 1. It seems that at that time there were between 900 and 1000 employees as can be seen in the photograph in the section of the book on night watch man etc.

Even though machines were by that time used in almost every process, every process was still very labour intensive. In the photographs in the centenary brochure (1906) there are rows of women sitting burnishing. At the same time the firm was offering thousands of products that could be produced to order in silver, EPNS or pewter for use in almost every room in the home. Many of these were kitchen implements or tableware but others were both functional and decorative such as candlesticks, lamps and hairbrushes. There was also quite a large department producing equipment for country sports particularly the 'hunting and shooting' market. These products were world renowned as can be seen from the prize medals awarded at exhibitions (1) all over the world:

London 1851	two bronze medals
Paris 1855	one silver medal
London 1862	two bronze medals
Akola, India	one silver medal
Chili 1875	one silver medal
Sydney 1878	one bronze medal
Melbourne 1880	one bronze medal
Calcutta 1883-4	one gold and two silver medals
Paris 1889	one bronze medal

Collectables
The rich have always collected valuable works of art and old country houses are full of them. Of all the things that Dixon's produced the most

highly collected in the modern era are those associated with the designer Christopher Dresser. It is his name that makes a teapot that cost about £2 to make in the 1880s-90s sell for £80,000 or more today despite the fact that it is made from electroplated nickel silver. Forgotten are the modellers and pattern makers and the silversmith's of Dixon's whose craftsmanship turned his drawings into something real and lasting. However like many great designers and artists, it was to be many years before anyone recognised his genius and sadly no one at Dixon's as far as I can tell ever did. If someone in management had, might this have been a way to enable a small firm at least to survive? Moorcroft's the Burselm pottery manufacturers seem in this era to survive mostly by producing products for the collector's market.

Quality Pieces and Trophies

It seems that it was in the 1930's that Dixon's became world famous for producing special pieces that were to mark special occasions or sporting events. What criteria can be used for saying this was the pinnacle of their achievements? Uniqueness, design, cost, craftsmanship and having listed these things how do you define each of them? It also true to say that for pieces like the Blue Riband and the Masters' golf trophy, specifications were given to Charles Holliday. As a designer he did not have a blank page. He had to take those specifications and translate them into a design that was achievable by craftsman using silver or gold. All I can say is that the pictures of these objects d'art leave me feeling in awe of the combined skill of those who worked on them. In pieces that I have seen I admire the line, the elegance, the little touches that relate the piece to the occasion, event or the person. It is integral to the design and never overstated. What I think we can be sure of is that those who from the 1930's to the 1970's were producing such work were doing so by building on the skill, experience and expertise of the previous generations of master crafts people. In this sense the zenith could have been towards the end of the firm's existence. Part of the problem was that such pieces were hardly profitable in economic terms and production of more basic products on which the survival of the firm depended was already in decline. Following World War 2 this accelerated.

Conclusion

If a firm such as Dixon's exists to manufacture products which cover all costs and produce sufficient profit for reinvestment and shareholders, one would really have to say that the zenith was between 1900 and 1914. At that time they had a reputation for high quality goods and they supplyed the great retail outlets of the day such as Harrod's. They also made cutlery engraved with the hotel's crest and name for establishments like the Savoy in London. Last but not least they made products that were sold all over the world to ordinary people and a visit to any antique fair or indeed to Ebay will usually yield in any one week a Dixon's piece often available in EPNS for very little cost.

One of the most poignant statements that I have come across is a cutting in the archives from the EmGas magazine of Spring 1975 which says: *with a healthy £800,000 per annum turnover, a workforce which is proud of belonging to the Dixon 'family' and an increasing awareness on behalf of the general public of quality tableware this is one firm that could be going strong in the year 2006'* (2)

Sources

1   Centenary Souvenir Booklet 1906
2   Sheffield archives, Dixon's B447 Papers of Milo Dixon, Memoranda book 1962-73

Memorial to James Willis Dixon (second generation) today still in Wadsley Church